The Home-Based Business Accelerator

by

Daniel J. Oase, MBA

Assistant Professor

Santiago Canyon College

This book is dedicated to my daughter Björk, who waited two years longer.

Contents

Preface

The "Big WHY?"

How to Find and Do Work You Love

New Business Concepts

Identifying Unmet Needs in the Marketplace

Scaling Your Business in Five Dimensions

Forms of Business Ownership

Generating Profits

e-Commerce, Leadgen, and Publishing

Including the Family

Financial Statements

The Home-Based Business Accelerator

Obtaining Startup Funding

Creating a Proposal for a Prospective Customer

Patents, Trademarks, and Protecting Your Intellectual Property

Playing the Endgame

Preface

This book is designed to help you find and do the work you love at your own home-based business. This how-to guide will show you all the tips and techniques you need to get started. It is designed for readers with little or no business experience who are thinking about starting a business, or are in the early stages of forming one.

This is a different kind of a textbook; this is a book that is **not** filled with fancy artwork, graphs, and images galore. Rather, this book is written for the type of person who wants to start a successful business and get started on a shoestring budget.

To that end, I have included a balance of business theory, applications, and exercises to guide you along your journey to business ownership. If you already have a business, this book can help you expand it, or if you haven't even started, this book can help get that process going. My aim is to help you work at home and make money. If we can do that, this book has served its purpose. Good luck!

Chapter 1:

The "Big WHY?"

Why do you want to start a home-based business? When you start building a business, you do not begin with the business; you begin with you. Before getting underway, it is important to be able to tell someone why you want to do it, preferably in less than thirty seconds. If you cannot answer it in a few sentences, keep trying until you can.

Do you want to have the freedom to set your own schedule? Be your own boss? Are you drawn to the potential of an unlimited source of income? These are great short-term motivators, but what you need to stay in the game for the long haul is a reason that you can draw from, tap into, when times are tough. Tell me why is it that you want to own and operate a home-based business more than anything else? That is the "Big WHY."

Forbes reports that home-based businesses are becoming the fastest growing form of business start-ups[1]. Owning and operating a company out of your home allows for flexibility and lower expenses since it is likely that you will not need to rent or buy office or warehouse space. Working at home will require self-discipline, but the benefits can be substantial especially when you are getting started.

---

[1] "The Top 6 Benefits Of Starting A Home-Based Business."

One of the most fundamental questions we must answer is the difference between simply working at home and owning a home-based business. These concepts are related and you will benefit from reading this book regardless of which type you prefer; but there needs to be a distinction made early on. When you work at home, you perform services for an employer in exchange for a paycheck. When you own and operate a home-based business, that employer is you. The main difference between the two in which we will explore is that the home-based business owner can benefit from all the rewards and unlimited earnings potential that business ownership has to offer. Employees do not take on the same risks, or have access to the same rewards, as the business owner does. Think about your future paychecks for a moment: do you want to sign the front, or the back of those paychecks? Your answer to that question sets the stage for how you proceed to answer the "Big WHY."

To assist you in searching for your answer, here are some of the key benefits[2] of owning a home-based business. Reflect on these reasons and complete the exercise at the end of this chapter.

1. **Commute Less, Work More**

    Would it be nice to create an extra hour or two of work time each day? Many employees spend approximately an hour traveling to and from work each day. Working at home can give you the opportunity to shave that time off your commute and reinvest it in more productive operations at your home office.

2. **Grow Rapidly**

    When you rent or own office space, your business is limited to the space you are provided. If you grow rapidly, you may need to negotiate the terms of your lease; or if you need to downsize, you may not be able to do so

---

[2] "7 Ways To Enjoy The Process Of Starting Your Own Business."

quickly if you are locked in a long-term lease. Working from home gives you flexibility to expand or contract your operation depending on how things are going.

3. **Tax Benefits**

   Speaking to a tax advisor about the tax benefits of operating a home office can be worthwhile. If you qualify, you may be able to deduct a portion of your home's expenses, such as mortgage interest, property taxes, utilities and repairs and maintenance, against your business income. Your aim should be to enter the conversation with a qualified tax advisor to discuss how to include those expenses to minimize tax liability

4. **Flexible Schedule**

   Entrepreneurs with children or other obligations are often drawn to home-based businesses because of the need to work at night or first thing in the morning while the kids are asleep. Technology such as smart phones, video conferencing, instant messaging, and email allow you to interact with your customers and suppliers at any time of the day or night. This provides the opportunity to more easily accommodate customers from anywhere in the world.

5. **Lower Costs of Doing Business**

    Working from your home-based office keeps your costs low because you are not renting office space or phones or paying for office utilities; you will probably tap into the services you already use when you get started. Since you are not commuting, you will save on transportation costs such as gas and depreciation of your car. This can give your business a competitive advantage because you can adjust your pricing based on reduced fixed costs. In other words, you can lower your prices a bit, or you can keep prices the same and earn higher profits.

6. **Fulfillment**

   Operating your own business can be a very rewarding and gratifying experience. It does not matter how big or how small your idea is; when you do something you're passionate about, your journey to success can be much easier and fulfilling.

7. **Do Something You Love**

   Entrepreneur Judith Humphrey suggests to start with something you love—you will be spending a lot of time with the business so you have to love its product or service.

The questions below are designed to help you arrive at the answer to your "Big WHY." Ideally, your business venture should maximize the overlap between what you are good at, what you enjoy doing, and that you will get paid to do. Later chapters will explore how to identify needs in the marketplace and position your business products or services to meet the needs of your customers. But for now, continue to focus on you and why you want to do this.

I am good at:

_____

_____

_____

_____.

I enjoy doing:

_____

_____

_____

_____

_____.

I can get paid to do:

_____

_____

_____

_____

_____.

I want to start a home-based business because:

_____

_____

_____

_____

_____.

Chapter 2:

How to Find and Do the Work You Love

Motivational speaker Scott Dinsmore gave an electrifying TedTalk about how to find and do the work you love[3]. This chapter will begin by diving into a few key takeaways from his talk. According to Dinsmore, your work will not be as satisfying if you only go to an office to build your resume. This is much like something Warren Buffett was fond of saying:

There comes a time when you ought to start doing what you

want. Take a job that you love. You will jump out of bed in

the morning. I think you are out of your mind if you keep

taking jobs that you don't like because you think it will look

good on your resume. Isn't that a little like saving up sex for

---

[3] Dinsmore, Scott. "How to Find Work You Love." Ted.com

your old age?

If you are currently working, ask yourself, "Why am I doing the work that I am doing?" If you are not working, ask yourself, "Why do I want to do this work?" To help you answer these questions, there are exercises below to use as a lens to help you identify what you are looking for. This is particularly important before starting a home-based business because if you do not know what you're looking for, you'll have trouble finding it.

When I wake up in the morning, I love to:

_____

_____

_____

_____

_____.

The things that people thank me for are:

_____

_____

_____

_____

_____.

Five years from today, I want to be:

_____

_____

_____

_____

_____.

I think I can solve these problems:

_____

_____

_____

_____

_____.

How do you find a problem to solve? Start by turning inward to things you are familiar with, such as travel, sports, entertainment, arts and crafts, and so on. What are the challenges that surround the things you like to do? Is there a more convenient or comfortable way to travel by airplane? Could you create a more comfortable pillow that fits around a passenger's neck more easily than the ones currently offered? Once you know, take the idea to people you know—people who will tell you what they really think—and ask if they would use it. If you get to that point, you have the inkling of a new product.

Next, you should carefully consider the true value it offers the customer. Your value proposition is what makes your product or service attractive to the consumer. When you first begin, it is common to overestimate the value of your solution, and for your customer to overvalue the solution they currently use by as much as 900%[4]. In other words, to convince a consumer to switch to your product or service, you should aim to convince him or her that it is *ten times better* than what that customer is currently using.

Understanding this bias and how it affects your customer's decision to purchase your offerings is essential. For example, a customer may pay a fee to activate a new service, spend time learning how to use a new software program, or figure out what do with a DVD collection when switching to a streaming video service. Many customers view these expenditures of money, time, and effort as losses, and this perception can cause them to stick with what they're already doing.[5]

---

[4] Gourville, J. T.
[5] Applegate, L.

Chapter 3:

New Business Concepts

You have decided to start a home-based business for good reasons. Now you may be wondering how to turn that business concept into something that generates cash flow. We will explore three basic types of new business ideas: 1) ideas to enter new markets, 2) ideas based on new technologies, or 3) ideas that offer new benefits. Each of these has unique features and benefits. Let's take a look at each of them.

If you provide a product or service that does **not** exist in your particular market but **does** exist elsewhere, you have a new market idea. For example, you will provide something that customers can only get somewhere far away. An import/export business may fit into this model. This approach has tremendous potential and the upside is large. Uncertainty and risk are reduced because the concept has been proven in another market; you are just bringing it home, so to speak.

New technology ideas, on the other hand, operate in areas of much more uncertainty. The product and the market are untested. There is no definitive model of success or anything to base it on except intuition. Your technology needs to be approximately ten times more valuable in the eyes of the consumer than what (s)he currently uses; it needs to be feasible to introduce to the market within your budget, and the market needs to be large enough to reward your efforts. Your business needs to be flexible to quickly respond if an idea does not catch on and try a different approach that may be more effective.

Ideas that are based on offering customers better products and services, or better ways of doing things they already do are called new benefit ideas. A self-driving car would be an example of this type of model (and it also has characteristics of other models). A solar-powered lawn mower would be another example of this model. In essence, it is creating something that can perform a function more effectively than other products or services on the market.

Where will these ideas come from? Most entrepreneurs get ideas from prior work experience. For example, they work at a regular job and discover an unmet customer need, or they find a new process or product that is more efficient and more valuable to the customer than what is currently available. Other sources of ideas may come from hobbies, and sometimes, ideas happen accidentally.

The value of your personal network is huge, especially when it comes to generating and refining new ideas. For example, you may ask a supplier within your network if (s)he is interested in partnering with you or with customers whose needs are unmet by other businesses. In practice, this would be something like a designer sunglass supplier who wanted to distribute eyewear to consumers near your home. Your business would purchase large quantities of those sunglasses and sell them to your local customers.

Hobbies are a great source of business ideas. For example, if you work at a regular office job, but you make jewelry at home as an after-hours hobby, you may want to transition into making and selling jewelry as a full-time profession. Be cautious, as you may no longer enjoy your hobby due to constant pressure to be faster, cheaper, and profitable. Thus your decision to convert a hobby into a business should be made carefully. Here are some questions[6] to ask yourself before converting a hobby:

---

[6] Landau, C.

- Will you still enjoy it when you have to produce things according to deadlines?
- Will you enjoy doing it when financial pressures mount and you need to speed up production to pay rent?
- Are you really committed to this hobby?
- Are you inspired by a challenge? You will be filling many roles when you start your business: sales, customer service, accounting, operations, and so on. These functions take a lot of time, which will be one of your scarcest resources.
- Can you sell "yourself" or the things you create? Personal branding is as important as marketing the product. Keep your social media profiles updated and participate in your community.

I have provided additional exercises to help you turn ideas into new home-based business concepts. These stem from the notion that great ideas can spring and create profit from existing hobbies

I would love to teach someone how to:

_____

_____.

I could write something each week about what is happening in:

_____

_____.

I can easily fix:

_____

_____.

Chapter 4:

Identifying Unmet Needs in the Marketplace

After you have assessed the "why?" of starting a home-based business, it is time to identify unmet needs in the marketplace and align your product offerings to meet those needs. There is a marketing formula for making money: [what a customer wants] -- [what a customer gets] = opportunity to make money. Unmet needs in the market are the things your customers want in which your business can provide. For example, if you identify that a substantial number of customers want personalized mouse pads, but current vendors only provide pre-made mouse pads, your business can profit by producing custom mouse pads.

The process of identifying the new business venture opportunity involves several stages: associating, questioning, observing, networking and experimenting[7]. During the associating phase, you will connect seemingly unrelated questions, problems, or ideas. Then you will ask questions that may challenge conventional wisdom and the status quo to compete against the competition. You will observe common behaviors and demands of your customers. One of the most valuable, yet underutilized, sources of ideas is your network, the people you know who can share diverse perspectives, expertise, and experiences. Finally, you will constantly experiment to determine what will work. Thomas Edison was fond of saying that he never failed; he just found thousands of ways that things didn't work.

---

[7] Applegate, L.

When people think of my product, they also think of:

_____

_____

_____

_____

_____.

Instead of using my product, people who would use it are currently:

_____

_____

_____

_____

_____.

When observing my prospective customers, I have noticed that they like:

_____

_____

_____

_____

_____.

The five people whom I can talk to that will give me diverse perspectives or experiences are:

_____

_____

_____

_____

_____.

To test my assumptions and "learn by doing," I will

_____

_____

_____

_____

_____.

Chapter 5:

Scaling Your Business in Five Dimensions

Scaling your business is one of your top long-term goals. Scaling describes a company's ability to grow without being hampered by its structure or available resources[8]. Technology has empowered businesses to grow in many new ways, changing the way customers are acquired, and transactions are conducted. For example, technology companies grow rapidly and can often scale more quickly than other types of businesses, resulting in new opportunities for entrepreneurs to meet needs in the marketplace quickly. These companies are able to scale quickly because they typically carry low inventory, or use a software as a service (SaaS) model of producing goods and services. Moreover, companies with low operating overhead and little to no burden of warehousing and inventory do not need many resources or infrastructure to grow rapidly[9].

---

[8] Investopedia
[9] Investopedia

Your home-based business does not need to be related to the technology industry to scale. Customer acquisition, for example, can be streamlined through tools such as social media and digital advertising. It has also become easier to use than in the past. Even dog walking businesses can implement digital advertising strategies to increase signups for services, increasing customer bases and revenue potential.

When developing your business scaling strategy, focus on the following five areas: customers, products, team, financials, and the business model. Success or failure in one or more of these dimensions can make or break your ability to scale up your business.

1. **Customers** - Before creating your marketing budget, think about the lifetime value of the customer. In other words, if you operate a mobile car wash business, you need to estimate how many times a customer will use your service during the life of your business relationship. Multiply that by the amount (s)he spends on a car wash

and the result is the simplified customer lifetime value (LTV). For example, if you charge $10 for a car wash, and your customer average one wash per month for three years, then the lifetime value of that customer is $10 x 12 X 3 = $360. That is the maximum amount of money you should spend to acquire customers without losing money (if you had no other expenses!). A main reason businesses fail to scale is due to high customer acquisition costs, which result in lower profits.

2. **Products** - Part of the excitement of developing a new product is the ... PRODUCT. However, people do not pay for a product; they pay for a solution to a problem. If their car won't start, they buy a battery because it solves the problem. One of the greatest causes for product failure is the lack of attention to solving a problem. Furthermore, it is easy for designers to be carried away

with nice-to-have features that do not solve the customer's essential problems.

3. **Team** - It is easy to get carried away when hiring specialists before they are needed. Although they may be essential in time, customer service reps, marketing managers, product managers need to be hired in a timely manner when business cash flows are sufficient to support those positions. When building your home-based business, you will probably handle all those functions, so be prepared!

4. **Financials** - The problem with starting a business is not that it costs three times as much and takes twice as long as you thought it would; the problem is that it's the other way around. This stems from three causes. The first may simply be an overly optimistic cost estimate. Occasionally, underestimating is politically motivated to

ensure project approval. In other words, you may want to get the business off the ground so intensely that you miscalculate your expenditures. For example, you want high-speed Internet for your business, and your cost estimate is equivalent to your home Internet, say $49 per month. Later you call to have it installed, only to discover that Internet service for businesses is $199 per month. Similarly, for credit card processing services, you estimate the bank will charge $0.95 + 2.95% per transaction, and then you discover that it also charges an $89 monthly minimum activity fee. The list goes on. Second, any schedule delays inevitably translate into additional costs. Third, physical results may differ from the planning stages. Many new entrepreneurs have difficulty understanding plans and specifications (especially with website and graphic design); you may seek changes and edits that may incur significant implementation costs. These additional costs could be eliminated if specifications were made in the initial planning stage[10].

5. **Business Model** - When faced with financial pressures, a home-based business owner may feel tempted to focus on profit maximization prematurely. During the start-up and the growth stages of the business, operations will be lean, and profits will need to be reinvested for business growth. As an owner, you will need to constantly make small investments throughout the life of your business, and adapt the business model to a changing market.

---

[10] Wideman, Max.

Chapter 6:
Forms of Business Ownership

Once you have a picture of what types of goods or services your business will provide, you need to consider what form of business ownership will be the best fit for your goals. Approximately 800,000 new businesses are formed each year in the United States, and the way you form your business can make a big difference in your long-term success. The three main forms of business ownership are sole proprietorships, partnerships, and corporations.

A **sole proprietorship** is a business that is owned, and usually managed, by one person; it is the most common form of business ownership. This form of business is relatively easy to establish. In many cases, you may just need to obtain a business license and you will be ready to open shop. Whether you're starting a business from home or looking to move into a home office, it's important not to overlook the fact that your business is still subject to license and permit laws. A few types of licenses and permits will be introduced later in this chapter.

A **partnership** is a form of business with two or more owners. In a general partnership, the partners are jointly responsible for the debts of the firm, regardless of who was responsible for causing those debts. For example, if you establish a general partnership and the other partner makes purchases using the business accounts, you are both equally responsible for the payments. The upside is that partnerships tend to be more likely to succeed than sole proprietorships, but sharing profits and liabilities can lead to conflict among partners. There are other forms of partnerships, such as limited partnerships (LPs) and limited liability partnerships (LLPs), which have special structures of their own.

A conventional (C) **corporation** is a state-chartered legal entity with authority to act and have liability separate from its owners. That means is if the corporation is named as the defendant in a lawsuit, it may be responsible for paying the damages. The stockholders are not liable for the debts of the corporation beyond the money they invest. In other words, say you were a stockholder in Apple and invested $10,000. The following year Apple got sued and went bankrupt because it lost a $100,000,000,000 lawsuit. Your liability would stop at the $10,000 you invested, not the full amount of the lawsuit. Like partnerships, there are other variations of the corporation, which you can carefully consider when selecting the form of your business.

Regardless of which form of business ownership you establish, you may need to obtain a business license. Importantly, a business owner may be required to carry a license so revenue can be tracked for taxation purposes. Businesses that sell taxable goods or services also need a sales tax license or permit[11]. Licenses and permits are also used to protect the public and are required in federally regulated industries (aviation, firearms, alcohol businesses, etc.). Other industry licenses signify specific expertise. For example, if you run an in-home hair styling business, you will need the same professional license as a main street salon. Regulations vary based on industry and location, therefore it is important to have the correct information before you start doing business at your home. Caron Beesley at the Small Business Administration compiled a list[12] of the types of licenses and permits your business may require:

---

[11] Beesley, C.
[12] Beesley, C.

1. **General Business Licenses** – Your city or county government website can help you obtain one. It is an annual license or permit that legally entitles you to operate a business within that location. A small application fee is typically required.

2. **Professional and Trade Licenses** – State governments require certain businesses or industries to obtain professional/occupational licenses, such as a child care operation or real estate license. You can contact your state's business license office – or check the website – for a complete list of occupations that require licensing.

3. **Home Occupation Permit** – Many city and county zoning and planning agencies require all home-based businesses to obtain a Home Occupation Permit. If a permit is not required in your city, the zoning office can determine if your neighborhood is zoned for the home business activity you plan to conduct. If your area is not zoned for your type of business, you may need

to file for a variance or conditional-use permit. This guide, Zoning Laws for Home-Based Businesses, has additional information about zoning laws for home-based businesses.

4. **Sales Tax Permit** - If you intend to sell taxable goods or services (online or offline), you may be required to collect state and local sales taxes from your customers. If you sell products in a state that charges a sales tax or levies a gross receipt or excise tax on businesses, you may need to apply for a tax permit or register with your state revenue agency. This blog explains the process of obtaining a permit and collecting sales tax: Sales Tax 101 for Small Business Owners and Online Retailers.

5. **Health and Safety Permits** – Depending on your location and industry, you may need either a permit or an inspection from your local fire department, especially if your business requires the use of flammable materials or involves assembly of

several people in one location, such as a child care business.

Air and water pollution caused by businesses are also monitored in some communities. You can check with your state environmental protection agency if any of these regulations are applicable. Health Department permits are typically issued by your county government, pending an inspection of the business premises if you plan to sell food to the public or to other businesses. Additional permits may be required for food service or food preparation depending on your state.

6. **Sign Permits** – Some cities and towns have sign ordinances in effect that restrict the type, size, or location of signs placed on your property. Check with local authorities.

7. **Construction Permits** – If you need to make structural changes to your property to accommodate your in-home business, environmental and building permits may be required

for construction. It is a good idea to check with your local government's building and planning department before undertaking any construction.

8. **Check with Your Home Owner's Association (HOA)** – If you live in a planned residential or complex and have an HOA, your HOA won't specify particular licenses or permits. However, it can restrict the type of business activities you conduct in your home.

Based on my business model, the form of business most appropriate is

_____
_____
_____.

My business will require the following permits or licenses

_____

_____

_____.

One of your key responsibilities for the new business is obtaining an Employer Identification Number, or EIN, from the IRS. An EIN is a unique nine-digit number that identifies your business for tax purposes. It's similar to a Social Security number but is meant for business related items only. As a business owner, you'll need an EIN to open a business bank account, apply for business licenses and file tax returns. It is helpful to apply for one as soon as you start planning your business. This will ensure there are no delays in obtaining the appropriate licenses or financing in which you may need to operate. You can apply for one directly on the IRS website at www.irs.gov. According to the IRS[13], if you answer "yes" to any of the questions below, you will probably need an EIN:

---

[13] "Small Business/Self-Employed Topics"

- Do you have employees?
- Do you operate your business as a corporation or a partnership?
- Do you file any of these tax returns: Employment, Excise, or Alcohol, Tobacco and Firearms?
- Do you withhold taxes on income, other than wages, paid to a non-resident alien?
- Do you have a Keogh plan?
- Are you involved with any of the following types of organizations?

    -Trusts

    -IRAs

    -Exempt Organization

    -Business Income Tax

    -Returns

    -Estates

    -Real estate mortgage investment conduits

    -Non-profit organizations

-Farmers' cooperatives

-Plan administrators

If you're new to business, you may not be familiar with navigating the tax environment. First ask yourself which tax laws will initially impact your business? You may assume that your tax obligations kick in once you start making a profit. Not necessarily. Each business is different. For example, some states have a minimum tax to operate an LLC. At the time of this writing, California charges $800 LLC tax per year, even if your business loses money!

Also, if you hire employees, you'll have payroll tax obligations. If you operate a retail business, there is sales tax to deal with. Then there are quarterly estimated tax payments (the self-employed equivalent of withholding). To help you navigate the business tax landscape, here is a quick overview of key tax obligations that may impact you, courtesy of Caron Beesley from the Small Business Administration.

How you legally structure your business will affect your tax situation. For example, if the business is an LLC, the LLC will be taxed separately from the owners. On the other hand, sole proprietors report their personal and business income taxes on the same form (Form 1040).

At the state level, you will encounter several tax obligations – sales tax, property tax, income tax, unemployment insurance tax, and more. The SBA offers more information on how your business structure determines your tax obligations (plus links to the necessary forms and portals for registering your business with the right tax authority).

An Employer Identification Number (EIN) is the business equivalent of your social security number. It is required of businesses that have employees, operate as a corporation or partnership, and other obligations. Sole proprietors do not need an EIN and can operate using their social security number.

It is easily to overlook paying estimated taxes, especially if you are new to business and previously had income tax payments automatically withheld. Each quarter, self-employed business owners must estimate their federal and state income tax payment and send a check to the IRS and their state treasury. This "pay-as-you-go" model applies to sole proprietors, partners, and S Corporations who expect to pay $1,000 in income tax in one year. The threshold drops to $500 for Corporations[14].

To help you calculate your estimated tax, check out the IRS Estimated Tax guide. Consult your state's treasury office to receive the appropriate tax voucher or pay online.

It is very important that you set aside sufficient capital to meet your estimated tax payments or you risk a cash flow problem. Don't forget to keep good records of your income and expenses. The latter can be used to offset how much estimated tax you pay.

Sales tax applies to certain retail products (rarely services). If your business has a physical presence in a state, such as a store, office or warehouse, you must apply for a sales tax permit and collect applicable state and local sales tax from your customers. That tax is then passed on to your state revenue office on a monthly or quarterly basis. Determining whether your business qualifies as having physical presence in a particular state (say, if you own a warehouse in Virginia but sell your

---

[14] Beesley, C.

services in Pennsylvania) and the implications on sales tax collection can be confusing. Certain states are exempt from sales tax, including Alaska, Delaware, Hawaii, Montana, New Hampshire and Oregon.

If you start your business and immediately have employees on payroll, you will need to withhold Social Security (FICA), Medicare and federal and state income taxes from their salaries. You must also match and pay your employees' FICA and Medicare taxes in addition to each employee's tax. The "IRS Employment Taxes" guide has all the information you need to understand how to deposit and report employment taxes, key due dates, and more.

Bringing on a self-employed contractor brings additional tax ramifications, especially if your business accidentally or deliberately misclassifies that individual as an employee.

Since you will be operating the business from your home, you need to be aware of the property tax climate. Your local government (town, city, or county) may collect property tax for business assets such as vehicles, computer equipment, software, and more. Likewise, if you do business in a commercial real estate location, the state will collect property tax on it. Check with your local tax authority to determine what is required to register your property and the process for assessing and making payments.

Chapter 7:

Generating Profits

The distance between a business and a hobby can be measured by the cash flow it generates. Ideas can be passing thoughts, intellectually stimulating thought-exercises, fun projects, potentially profitable, or a sustainable competitive advantage that can be monetized such that it becomes a business. One of my mentors was fond of saying "I'm a salesman; I don't do unpaid consulting." What he meant is that he was not calling on customers to share good ideas and timely information; rather, he was in the business of exchanging his solutions for cash. At the outset of planning a home-based business, your mindset should be on your monetization strategy for converting your idea into a profitable venture. Earlier in the book, you learned about identifying unmet needs in the marketplace, and now you will explore ways to generate the profitable ideas to satisfy those needs.

Once you identify a need that your customers have that is not being met, how will your solution be different from the alternatives? What resources and capabilities do you have at your disposal? Your idea can gain traction in the marketplace by occupying an opportunity space, where your product fills a gap that no other product can. How much will it cost to produce your goods or services?

Pricing decisions are among the most important stages in business planning. The prices you charge will directly impact the amount of profit you make. If you charge too much, your sales volume will be low and it might not cover your overhead. On the other hand, if you don't charge enough, you may not be profitable. You must strike a delicate balance by setting a price that is high enough to allow you to make a profit, and yet low enough to keep your merchandise affordable and competitive. So how much do you charge? Below are some commonly used pricing strategies to give you a starting point.

1. **Competitor-based pricing** is used to find out the prices that are currently acceptable to potential customers, given their choices with your competition. This is the method many new business owners use to begin pricing their products. This method is sometimes called market-based pricing. Be mindful that your competitors' cost structures may be different than your own; they may cost more or less to operate than it costs you. By following their pricing strategy, you are not guaranteed to make profits. If the price you charge does not cover costs, your business is going to lose money.

2. **Cost-plus pricing** is a method where you calculate the costs and add a profit percentage. Many construction companies use this method of estimating the costs of the project within the bid, and then add 10% profit and 10% overhead to the invoice. If you make the cost calculation just on materials and leave out other expenses, your business may not profit. Here are examples of several hidden costs that need to be priced into your goods and services: insurance, licensing, vehicles (including gas, repairs), electrical equipment, taxes, advertising, tools, supplies, rent, utilities, administrative costs (such as billing and scheduling), salaries, professional services (accountants and legal counsel).

3. **Industry norm pricing** is a method where you set prices according to what is normal in your industry. In some sectors, it is simply doubling or tripling the cost of the product sold. Unlike cost-plus pricing, you do not include your other business expenses into these cost calculations. For example, if you sell skateboards and you know that the industry markup is 50%, then you can estimate the selling price based on the cost per skateboard. Many industries have significant variation between the markups; for example, the cost of a unique board signed by a professional might sell for 2-3 times more than a generic, off-brand board.

4. **Premium pricing** means setting the highest price target consumers will pay for a product or service, given their needs. Variations of this strategy are known as market skimming, where you introduce a new product, such as an ultra-high resolution television, for a very high price that is relative to other products in the market. For example, 48-inch screen televisions may be selling for $500, but you are the first one to market with a 48-inch television in ultra-high resolution model. You may set your price to $1,750 at first to sell it to the customers who want it immediately, and then lower your price over time to capture more of the market and achieve higher sales volume. Your strategy would be to focus on a specific market segment, then appeal to a larger audience when your product gains traction in the marketplace.

Let's take a detailed look at pricing from a retail standpoint. Retail stores usually use a markup between two to three times the cost. For example, if they buy a shirt for $3, they usually sell it between $6 and $9. Although there are no concrete rules for pricing products, each industry has a range in which it operates. Accounting, tax preparation, bookkeeping and payroll services firms generate an average net profit margin of 19.6%. This industry includes not only offices of Certified Public Accountants and tax preparers, which typically generate even higher margins than the category average, but also firms providing back office services such as payroll and financial records[15]. Since markup is figured as a percentage of the sales price, when you double your cost, it means you have a 50% markup. For example, if your cost on an item is $2, your selling price will be $4, and 50% of $4 is $2, which is your markup.

If you plan on selling products from your home, you need to be familiar with the costs associated with e-commerce or retail. When calculating your net margin, you must include all costs to calculate the correct figure. For example, say you achieve sales of $50,000 and earn a net profit of 4%. It does not mean that you only marked up your products by 4%. In reality, net profit is calculated after overhead expenses (rent, administration,

---

[15] Biery, M.

utilities, etc.) have been subtracted from your gross profit, which may have been 50%.

While it is true that higher volumes can make up for lower prices, unless you can sell as much as a Wal-Mart, you will almost certainly need at least a 50% markup to survive in a small home-based business. Although doubling the price may sound excessive—and you may want to discount heavily to acquire market share or make a name for yourself—it does not result in excessive profits when you consider the expenses for rent, taxes, insurance, supplies, and labor.

If you cannot compete at full price, you may need to discount your products occasionally. Be careful, however, not to discount too many items or you may find yourself trapped in a cycle of being a "low-cost" provider and you'll find nothing left for yourself at the end of the year. You can balance it by marking some items up slightly higher to compensate for the lower markups on others.

Here is a quick way to calculate your selling price:

Selling price = [(cost of item) ÷ (100 - markup percentage)] × 100

For example, assume an item costs you $10 and you want to use a markup of 35%.

The selling price would then be calculated as follows:

1. Selling price = [(10.00) ÷ (100 - 35)] × 100
2. Selling price = (10.00 ÷ 65) × 100 = $15.38

Do not multiply the cost by 35% and add that amount to the cost. That will produce a retail markup of 17.5%, not the desired 35%. Also, don't overlook freight costs in your cost of merchandise. If your competition will allow, add the freight cost before you apply the markup. Most of the time, however, you will simply add freight to the marked-up price, thus recovering only the cost of the freight.

Once you are clear about your pricing model and cost structure, you can run promotions and engage your customers in new ways. You will most likely accomplish this in some combination of digital and traditional methods. Your business will most likely need a website, and if you are an e-commerce business, a payment gateway such as credit card processing. Each bank has its own pricing structure for that service, which generally has a minimum monthly fee (often around $100), plus a flat rate ($0.45 - $2.00) and a percentage of the transaction (1% to 4%), just to process payments by credit card. For example, if a customer purchases a $100 skateboard from your website and pays by credit card, you may need to pay the bank $6 for that purchase, resulting in a $94 credit in your account. If the skateboard cost you $50, your margin went from 50% to 44%. If you only sold two skateboards that month on your website, you would not make enough profit to cover the $100 monthly fee for the credit card processing. Thus, when you are starting your business, it is very important to carefully plan how many units you can realistically sell during a promotion to cover your fixed costs and still generate a profit.

If it is financially possible to offer a promotion to attract customers, some of the least expensive ways to do so are through word-of-mouth and social media campaigns. The "buzz" you generate through word-of-mouth campaigns can come from customers telling other people about a great experience they had doing business with you. It may not cost you anything to reach out after a customer makes a purchase and ask him or her how everything is going. You may even offer some customers a discount in exchange for posting about their experience on social media accounts. Furthermore, you may consider making some promotional "giveaways," where people can demo your product for free if you interview them using it, and publish that video to YouTube. Below are some additional promotional considerations you can make.

I could run a contest to win a(n)

_____

_____

_____.

I could encourage my existing customers to refer their friends to me by

_____

_____

_____.

If I could donate a portion of my sales to charity, I would choose

_____

_____

_____.

If I could hold a customer appreciation event, I would include

_____

_____

_____

_____

_____.

Chapter 8:

e-Commerce, LeadGen, and Publishing Businesses

The main types of online business models are e-commerce, leadgen, and publishing. If your business operates online, it will probably fit into one or more of these categories. The e-commerce model is the most straightforward and most familiar. In this model, your business sells goods or services online. Amazon.com is one of the most recognizable examples of an e-commerce business. Leadgen businesses capture user information and sell it to someone else. Examples of leadgen businesses are sites like realtor.com, where users leave contact information if they are interested in a house and an agent responds. That website makes money on the back end by selling the user's information to a real estate agent who calls and attempts to sell the house to the user. A publishing business provides content, such as a blog, and sells advertising space on the site. LATimes.com is an example of a publishing business.

These types of businesses started emerging in the 1990s, when Internet service providers such as AOL, Prodigy, and CompuServe began providing access to the Internet via dialup connection, allowing users to browse the web at home. In those days, the business priority was to build a website. Establishing a web presence was the only thing the business owner needed to worry about. Once the site was live, it needed to be found. Companies like Yahoo!, Alta Vista, and Google came on the scene; then the next concern was search engine optimization (SEO), or making the website appear at the top of the search rankings. Now we are in a digital marketing atmosphere where social media and mobile technology are in the hands, heads, and hearts of most of your prospective customers. Your business needs to be present, visible, and provide content that customers value to the extent that they not only consume it, but also feel compelled to share with people they care about.

It has become increasingly difficult to break through the "noise" on the Internet because of the sheer volume of content and competition for virtual "face time" with the customer. How does this affect your business strategy? How do you plan to break through the clutter and reach your customer online? Below are some suggestions to help you navigate through it.

One of the ways to break through is by way of "viral marketing," which is advertising that reaches the masses quickly—like a viral epidemic. For example, your business produces a memorable YouTube video of someone using your product, and your customers share it with their friends; their friends share it with their friends, and so on. Small companies that use viral marketing usually advertise on various social networking sites. These sites include Facebook, Twitter and LinkedIn. When posting, they use personalized messages that are crafted and marketed to the likes of specific user segments, and embed videos to reach the vast user base of each site. Viral marketing is like a digital version of word-of-mouth advertising. That is, the average consumer usually tells several others about a positive buying experience. In social networking sites, interest in a product or a positive buying experience can catch on extremely fast. However, the messages that catch on are generally extraordinary. They can be humorous, informative, suspenseful, exciting, etc. You could also promote a contest where people have to identify people or animals using your products in new ways. Or you could write a blog that provides important tips for businesses if you run a consulting firm. There are many possibilities for creating great and shareable content.

Although this book is written primarily for the business-to-consumer (B2C) entities, there are some effective methods for business-to-business (B2B) entities to use as well. Unfortunately, B2B campaigns are often lackluster. Have you ever seen an advertisement in the transportation industry? The majority of ads feature just what you'd expect: trucks, airplanes, ships, ports and railroads. Running an advertisement that is too far from the norm is almost unheard of. Would that be acceptable in a B2C campaign? Not likely. The consumer would be lost and the brand would be, too. Successful marketing campaigns, whether they are B2B or B2C, need to stand out. What can you do as a home-based business owner do to do so? Take a good, hard look at the competition and gather some data. What are their strategies? Are you seeing similar campaigns and hearing the same messages repeatedly? Use the information you glean to arm yourself to think differently. In an operationally-driven industry like transportation, the marketing function takes significant input from operations[16].

---

[16] Nightingale., T.

Regardless of which business model you choose, your content should reflect your brand's image, and not be filled with sales pitches or marketing jargon. You need to engage with followers on a personal level and let them see the personality of your brand. Respond to mentions, answer questions, and talk with customers about what's on their mind. Use your social channels as an extension of your customer service strategy. In other words, it is no longer acceptable to just delete an unflattering remark by a customer on your Facebook page. You should address concerns, usually within one hour or less, to meet customers' expectations.

Your social media fans expect to see ads and sales messages in your timeline, but they will quickly tune you out if everything you post is a sales pitch about your latest and greatest offerings. Use data analytics, such as Google Analytics, to determine where customers are spending their time on your webpages, determine and discuss what is most important to your customers on social media. Your followers will appreciate your interest in their opinions about topics they care about, and not just an interest in the transaction itself.

One of the greatest challenges e-Commerce entrepreneurs face is figuring out what products to sell online. This is a huge decision that it can be paralyzing and in some cases off-putting, so the business never gets started in the first place. When you consider the cost of acquiring a large volume of inventory to receive sufficient price discounts, you may need to write a check for thousands of dollars. This mountainous choice typically ends up being the reason most people never actually start their online business. Let's take a look at some starting points for your e-Commerce business:

1. Start with your business name. Your first move is to choose a business name that no one else is using. You can conduct a corporate name search to ensure it is not already in use. If you are checking in California, you can use this website: http://kepler.sos.ca.gov/. Once you choose the name, check if the website domain name is available to register (provided you want to use the same name for your website as you use for your business).

You can check if the domain name is available by visiting this site:

https://www.godaddy.com/domains/domain-name-search

2. Ideally, your business name and domain name will be the same; but if the domain is not available, choose a related URL that is easy to pronounce and spell. It should be as short as possible, end in .com, and does not infringe on someone else's trademark. The design of your e-commerce site may be your biggest business expense. It must be visually appealing and functional. There are out-of-the-box e-commerce solutions such as Shopify to begin with, but you may require a custom-built site if your needs are more than basic.
3. After you establish these things, you will need to find the right vendors. With the substantial competition of selling products online, it is in your best interest to find the best quality and prices for your products, as well as materials

used to create those products[17]. Shop around until you find a long-term business vendor.

4. Start marketing as soon as possible. Sometimes you want to start marketing before your product is ready, or before you actually open shop. Even if you are not up and running, set up social media profiles and write blog content now so that you are not starting from scratch on opening day. You can set up a "coming soon" homepage on your website where interested customers can sign up to receive updates, using a tool like LaunchRock.

5. Get the right technology for your business. Technology can make your work easier. Before the launch of your e-commerce business, familiarize yourself and become proficient with customer relationship management (CRM), accounting, project management, and email marketing software.

6. Setup a commercial shipping account if you will be shipping a significant volume. For example, UPS has an

---

[17] Fishkin, R.

account feature that allows you to bill shipping charges and pay weekly rather than after each shipment, or schedule day-specific or daily pickups. You may even negotiate an advantageous shipping price. UPS often runs promotions for small businesses that may help you save more than 10% on shipping costs.

7. Build up your inventory and start selling! Make sure you have sufficient space to handle your inventory. Since you are operating out of a home office, it is wise to designate separate spaces for business and personal use. For example, if you report that you use your garage for business, but keep your personal fishing equipment in the same space, then it gets tricky. The same goes for using a room in your house; if you use your bedroom with a bed and television, then it is difficult to justify that the space is only being used for business purposes.

Unlike e-Commerce, leadgen businesses do not require inventory; however, your website must generate an "inventory" of leads to sell to your customers. If you enjoy doing extensive research to determine the types of leads that are in demand (e.g., insurance, mortgage, real estate), then this type of home-based business may be right for you. You will generally begin by building a website where you can drive targeted traffic to collect information from visitors. Also, you should include appealing site content for the visitors whom you are trying to capture information. For example, if you are blogging about home improvement and have an audience, you may want to generate leads for contractors to bid on household projects.

After you engage visitors with website content, you need to include a form for visitors to provide you their personal contact information. Also, provide questions related to the information you're collecting for your visitors to answer. The information you provide is usually in the form of blogs, videos, or free downloads, and is designed to draw homeowners to your site.

Once you have engaged visitors on your site, offer a free report download about ways to avoid the top 10 pitfalls of home improvement (e.g., runaway costs, discovering new problems, going over budget, etc.). When the visitor provides his/her personal contact information, he/she can download the report. In addition to the personal information, ask a question "When do you expect to complete this project?" Answers may include options such as (a) Just shopping, (b) 1-6 months, (c) 7 months – 1 year, and (d) Over 2 years. The question allows you to qualify the visitor, but also do a "give and take"; that is, if you are going to ask for the customer's information, you need to give him or her something in exchange. If you ask too many questions without giving the customer something in return, it will seem spammy and (s)he will leave your site.

After you have your lead generating system in place, turn your attention to attracting the clients who will buy the leads. Research, find, and contact clients who may be interested in the leads. You can do this offline by contacting potential customers via phone, email, or regular mail. This can also be done online in a similarly to how you collect leads on the "front end" of your business. In other words, build a website that focuses on services you provide as a lead generation company, and how it benefits the client (i.e. the contractor) to use your service.

As you gather lead information, you need a database to search for the leads and pull lists. Generally, database systems are software programs that can be loaded onto your computer. You can use it to input the lead information and search the database. It works by asking you to input the criteria the leads must fit. Then, based on the criteria, it will produce a list of the leads within your database. These are the leads you sell to your clients.

Building a website to gather leads can cost anywhere from $5 per month to $35 per month, depending on the website host and the website package you purchase[18]. Unless you are artistically inclined and have a knack for it, I suggest employing a graphic designer to work on your images. This would be a few hundred dollars well spent. In addition to the website, you may need to purchase the database software, which can cost a couple hundred dollars to a couple thousand dollars, depending on the software selected. Make sure your computer is compatible with the software you choose. It may be wise to run the database on a separate computer from your everyday computer, as many leadgen companies do. This may add a few hundred more dollars to your startup costs but it can be a worthwhile investment.

---

[18] Lorette, K.

The last online business model, publishing, is one where your content is your product. In other words, people visit your site to read your blog, watch your videos, etc. You make money by selling advertising space to businesses that want to run display advertisements on your pages. There are five major steps to building a publishing business.

First, you need to determine what you can publish that will engage an audience. Once you know that, you can determine what types of users to target. For example, if you are a great cook, you might want to dedicate your website to publishing recipes and cooking videos. If that is the case, you should attract visitors who are interested in cooking, and advertisers who sell things like cutlery, dishes, pans, etc.

Your website needs to be designed with the purpose of publishing content in mind. If you do not have experience building websites, there are several do-it-yourself platforms on the market such as Squarespace.com. You can adapt one of the templates to suit your purpose. Your font should be easy to read and professional. It is also helpful to use a variety of images so the pages are not text-heavy, which can be off-putting to some visitors. The more you clutter you have on your Internet publishing business site, the less likely you will generate heavy traffic[19]. Adding an analytics package, such as Google Analytics, is a must to present that data to a prospective advertiser when selling your advertising space.

Next, create a marketing plan to boost traffic to your site. The currency of your website is the number of unique visitors per day. The larger that number, the more leverage you will have to negotiate advertising rates on your website. One of the best ways to build traffic to monetize your website is by generating useful content that keeps visitors returning to your site. Link your site to your social media pages, submit it for directories in your category (for example, if your Internet publishing venture is about web design, then you want to be listed on directories with other web design businesses), and participate in "offline" conferences and events to showcase your site.

---

[19] Belcher, L.

You also need to optimize the website for the type of visitor you are trying to attract. For example, you should establish yourself as a thought leader in your field so people contact you first when they are looking for related information. Say you specialize in Cajun style cooking, have an extensive library of recipes in this niche, and also have a variety of recipes in closely related styles. Visitors will you come to you first for Cajun recipes, but can browse other offerings while on the site. You may invite bloggers from other sites to write a guest blog on your site. To improve your ranking on the search engine page, create a page that is highly relevant to what the visitor is searching for. It is your advantage to have specialized pages that cover certain topics in great detail and links from other credible websites that lead to your site. In other words, the search engine will reward your site if FoodNetwork.com provides links to your Cajun recipes. Your strategy, therefore, is to always provide the most relevant and credible content that also links from other major websites.

Which type of website will be right for your business? If you want to create a website on a zero budget, you might consider a free Strikingly site. It is great for beginners because it is easy to modify—with very little maintenance—and it will look good when it's done. If you want a blog for little to no money, you can build a WordPress.com blog. With either free option, your site will adopt a subdomain like yourname.strikingly.com or yourname.wordpress.com, which is a small price for an otherwise free site. Keep in mind that your visitors and the search engines will see that subdomain, which will definitely impact the way your prospective customers perceive the site. However, when you are just getting started, this may be the way to go.

If you are starting to sell services or products on your website or want to experiment with an e-store, Weebly or SquareSpace could be good choices. Weebly is less expensive (at the time of this writing, it starts at $4 per month), but the templates are arguably not as well-designed. Squarespace is a bit more expensive (starting at $8 per month), but looks sophisticated and professional.

I have verified that the domain name I have chosen

_____

_____is available.

My business is most similar to publishing / leadgen / e-Commerce model_____.

I have viewed the following "do it yourself" website generators

_____

_____

_____

_____

_____.

The website generator that is the best fit for my business is

_____

_____

_____.

Chapter 9:

Including the Family

Deciding to include your family in the home-based business should be carefully considered in regards to the way you want to operate the venture. For the purposes of this text, we look at family as the people you are tied to through your common biological, legal, cultural, and emotional history and your implied future together. Not to oversimplify too much, but we look at family as the bonds we share through blood or marriage. Family is the primary and, almost always, the most powerful system to which humans belong[20]. Thus, it is often the case that when the family is brought into the business, whatever happens to one system affects the other in some way. This may be one of the most important decisions you make in establishing your home-based business, and this chapter is designed to help you explore the implications of that decision carefully.

---

[20] McGoldrick, M.

Ariana Ayu at Inc. has compiled a list[21] of things to consider when starting a family business. We will explore some of these ideas in greater detail as we move through the analysis:

1. All the traditional rules of business still apply. This is now a business, even if it was once a hobby. You still need legal protection, solid strategies and business plans, operational systems, and competent partners. You also need it to make money.

2. It will definitely affect your relationships. You will notice right away that it's going to change the existing dynamic of how you relate to other family members, some for better and some for worse, but one things if for sure: you can't expect things to stay as they are. You will need to learn to have good boundaries and nurture your relationships with others in order to maintain long-term success.

---

[21] Ayu, Ariana.

3. I'm fond of saying that each ship must have a captain; someone has to be in charge. Even if you plan to share decision-making, someone needs to have the final say. Disagreements are inevitable, and if you're going to operate a real business (as in, not just a hobby), everyone needs to know who makes the final decisions. You may need to go so far as to have a written agreement that stipulates how decisions will be made when there is disagreement among family members.

4. This may be your dream, but it's not necessarily your family's dream. You will most likely have different levels of commitment to the business. Whether one (or more) of you is supporting the other's dream, or you are all excited about the mission at the start, things change. It is important to keep in mind that everyone on your family team may not feel exactly the same way you feel about the business, especially if your children are involved in the business.

5. Job titles (CEO, Owner, President, VP) may not be so clearly defined. If your youngest child is the best choice for the leader of the organization, it may be very difficult for him or her to manage older siblings, or even parents, who are in support roles. It may be equally difficult for older siblings and parents to have a younger child for a boss.

6. You have a lot to learn. If you assign tasks to family members based on need—rather than expertise—you all have a steep learning curve ahead of you. This may result in placing people in positions outside of their skill sets, and this can be one giant learning experience with growth and opportunity, or an expensive lesson, or somewhere in between. For example, if you assign the accountant role to someone to "keep it in the family," and (s)he is not skilled in that line of work, you may have more issues than if you brought in someone from the outside to do that for you.

7. You will need time off. If business is the main topic of conversation every time you're together, you may find that you lose sight of why you enjoyed the relationship in the first place. Make sure you spend time together (and apart) pursuing hobbies and interests that are not work-related. Consider banning work talk at the dinner table or on date night (if you can!).

8. Respect each other and communicate calmly and respectfully. When you work at a regular job, you can go home and complain to your family about your coworkers, but when your family members **are** your coworkers, you probably cannot do that anymore. Therefore, mutual respect and clear communication are critical. Calmly and respectfully dealing with issues when they arise (instead of letting small things build up into giant problems) helps maintain an atmosphere of professionalism that your entire company will benefit from.

9. Have strategies in place that explain how you will handle conflict. Plain and simple: when in doubt, plan it out.

When I operate my home-based business, the person in charge will be

_____
_____
_____.

The people handling accounting, management, marketing, and operations are

_____
_____
_____.

I will take time off by

_____

_____

_____.

When another family member and I disagree about something, we will

_____

_____

_____

_____

_____.

The benefit of family meetings is establishing a "council" that is the equivalent to a board of directors, providing a reliable forum for the education of family members about the state of the business, such as how it is doing financially, its strategy, and the challenges it faces. These council meetings can be a place for important discussions regarding business and family expectations for returns and tolerance for risk between the family and other stakeholders. These meetings can make the family stronger, and thoughtful discussion of each member's perspective on business strategy, succession planning, innovation, hiring practices, management, finance, etc., can increase trust, unity, and deeper commitment to goals. You will find that your family members will work harder to support something that they had an opportunity to create.

When you determine that it is time to start bringing in family members to business operations, it will be helpful to have a family employment policy in place. Below is a worksheet to help you define how other people will enter or exit your home-based business:

The purpose of the policy is to define the criteria and procedures that will be used to add or remove people from the business:

1. Will family members be required to meet the same criteria for hiring as non-family applicants?
2. Will family members be expected to meet the same performance standards as outsiders?
3. Will performance reviews be required for family members?
4. How will family members be supervised by non-family members, if at all?
5. How will family members' compensation be determined?

6. What types of education and experience will be required of family members?
7. How will family members communicate their desire to change positions or willingness to be promoted within the organization?

For additional guidance in the careful consideration of including the family in your home-based business, here are some questions to help you visualize the future state of the business for the next three years. These are large, very open-ended questions designed to help you think about the business on deeper levels:

1. What would you like to see as the core family business three years from now?
2. How would you like to see it managed?
3. What would you like to see as the governance structure?
4. How do you want to be involved specifically?
5. What are your expectations for financial returns?

6. How do you want your business to give back to your community?

Chapter 10:

Financial Statements

If you want to operate a successful home-based business, you must understand financial statements. These documents are essential to help you stay on course and can serve as checkpoints to exercise control over the direction your business. Although they are instrumental in the processes of filing taxes and applying for loans, they have a much larger significance.

The balance sheet and the income statement are two very common financial statements. The balance sheet is a snapshot of your business financials. It includes your business assets, liabilities and net worth. Net worth is also called owners' equity. For now, we will view assets as things your business owns, liabilities are the things it has to pay, and net worth is what's left over after the liabilities are subtracted from the assets.

For example, if you own a $10,000 copy machine (asset), but you owe the bank an $8,000 loan (liability), then your net worth is $2,000 ($10,000 - $8,000 = $2,000). The "bottom line" of a balance sheet must always include [assets = liabilities + net worth]. The items you list in your balance sheet can change on a daily basis, but they will always reflect business activities. If you look at a balance sheet carefully, you can get a lot of important information about how the business is performing. This information can help you can monitor your ability to collect the money people owe you, manage your inventory, and assess your ability to pay the people to whom you owe money.

Before you get to the point where you can start requesting significant startup funding, you need to paint a picture of what the business will look like financially. The liabilities and net worth sections on the balance sheet represent sources of funds. Sometimes, you exchange a portion of the ownership in your business for cash, and other times, you may apply for a bank loan to get the money you need to operate.

Assets represent the use of funds for something that your business needs. Most people are familiar with using cash to purchase something, like a computer, that they need to do something. In that example, you exchanged one asset (cash) for another asset (computer). However, it can become more complex as you augment your capital structure. For example, your business may receive cash (asset) in exchange for a liability (bank loan), in order to purchase a machine (asset). Although another step is added, the asset is still obtained and the balance sheet is still "in balance" as a result of that transaction.

Liabilities represent what your business owes to other people or to organizations, and net worth represents your investment in your business. In that sense, both creditors and owners are "investors" in the business; the only difference is the timeframe in which they expect repayment. Your creditors usually expect repayment from your business soon, but you may choose to pay yourself over your entire lifetime! Here are common items on the balance sheet and their definitions:

1. **Assets** - Anything of value that is owned or due to the business is included under the Asset section of a Balance Sheet.
2. **Current Assets** - Current assets mature in less than one year. They are the sum of:
    a. Cash
        i. Cash pays bills and obligations. Inventory, receivables, land, building, machinery and equipment do not pay obligations although these can be sold for cash to pay bills. If cash is inadequate or improperly managed, a business may become insolvent or forced into bankruptcy. Cash includes all checking, money market and short-term savings accounts. Learn more about how to develop a cash flow analysis for your business.
    b. Accounts Receivable (A/R)

i. Accounts Receivable (A/R): Accounts receivable are dollars due from customers. More specifically, inventory is sold and shipped, an invoice is sent to the customer, and cash is collected at a later time. The receivable exists for the time period between the selling of the inventory and the receipt of cash. Receivables are proportional to sales. As sales rise, the investment you must make in receivables also increases.

c. Inventory

i. Inventory: Inventory consists of the goods and materials a business purchases to resell at a profit. In the process, sales and receivables are generated. The business purchases raw material inventory that is processed (called work-in-process inventory) to be sold as finished goods inventory. For a business that sells a product, inventory is often the first use of cash. Purchasing inventory to be sold at a profit is the first step in making a profit. Selling inventory does not bring cash back into the business—it creates a receivable. Only after a time lag (equal to the receivable's collection period) will cash return to the business. It is important that inventory is well-managed so the business does not keep too much cash tied up in inventory, as this will reduce profits. At the same time, a business must keep sufficient inventory on hand to prevent stockouts (having nothing to sell). Insufficient inventory will erode profits and may result in the loss of customers.

d. Notes Receivable (N/R)

    i. Notes Receivable (N/R): N/R are claims due to the business as a result of the business making a loan, such as a promissory note. Notes receivable are claims due from one of three sources: customers, employees or officers of the business. Customer notes receivable are claims when borrowing customers fail to pay the invoice according to the agreed-upon payment terms. The customer's obligation may have been converted to a promissory note. Employee notes receivable may be for legitimate reasons, such as a down payment on a home, but the business is neither a charity nor a bank. If the business wants to help an employee, it can co-sign on a loan advanced by a bank.

An officer or owner borrowing from the business is the worst form of note receivable. If an officer borrows money from the business, it should be declared as a dividend or withdrawal, then be reflected as a net worth reduction. Treating it in any other way leads to possible manipulation of the business' stated net worth. Banks and other lending institutions often condemn this practice.

- e. Other Current Assets
    - i. Other Current Assets: Other current assets consist of prepaid expenses, other miscellaneous, and current assets.
3. **Fixed Assets** - Fixed assets represent the use of cash to purchase physical assets whose life exceeds one year, such as:

a. Land

b. Building

c. Machinery and equipment

d. Furniture and fixtures

e. Leasehold improvements

f. Intangibles

   i. Intangibles are assets with an undetermined life that may never mature into cash. For most analysis purposes, intangibles are ignored as assets and are deducted from net worth because the value is difficult to determine. Intangibles consist of assets such as:

      1. Research and development
      2. Patents
      3. Market research
      4. Goodwill
      5. Organizational expense

Intangibles are similar to prepaid expenses, which is the purchase of a benefit that will be expensed at a later date. Intangibles are recouped, like fixed assets, through incremental annual charges (amortization) against income. Standard accounting procedures require most intangibles to be expensed as purchased and never capitalized (include in the balance sheet). Purchased patents are an exception that may be amortized over the life of the patent.

4. **Other Assets**

    a. Other assets consist of miscellaneous accounts, such as deposits and long-term notes receivable from third parties. These are turned into cash when the asset is sold or when the note is repaid.

5. **Total Assets**

a. Total Assets represent the sum of all the assets owned by or due to a business.

6. **Liabilities and Net Worth**

   a. Liabilities and net worth are sources of cash listed in descending order from the soonest to mature obligations (current liabilities), to the net worth.

   b. There are two sources of funds: lender-investor and owner-investor. Lender-investor funds come from trade suppliers, employees, tax authorities and financial institutions. Owner-investor funds come from stockholders and principals who loan cash to the business. Both lender-investor and owner-investors have invested cash or its equivalent into the business. The only difference between the investors is the maturity date of their obligations and the degree of their nervousness.

7. **Current Liabilities**

a. Current liabilities are those obligations that will mature and must be paid within 12 months. These are liabilities that can create a business's insolvency if cash is inadequate. A satisfied set of current creditors is a healthy and important source of credit for short-term uses of cash (inventory and receivables). A dissatisfied set of current creditors can threaten the survival of the business. The best way to ensure creditors are satisfied is to keep their obligations current.

b. Current liabilities consist of the following obligation accounts:

   i. Accounts Payable (A/P): Accounts payable are obligations due to trade suppliers who have provided inventory, goods or services used in operating the business. Suppliers generally offer terms (just like you do for your customers), since the suppliers' competition offers payment terms. When possible, take advantage of payment terms because these will keep your costs down. If the business is paying its suppliers in a timely fashion, days payable will not exceed the terms of payment.

ii. Accrued expenses: Accrued expenses are obligations owed, but not billed such as wages and payroll taxes, or obligations accruing. These expenses can also be paid over a period of time, such as interest on a loan.

Accruals include wages, payroll taxes, interest payable and employee benefits accruals (i.e. pension funds). As a labor-related category, it should vary in accordance with payroll policy. For example, if wages are paid weekly, the accrual category should seldom exceed one week's payroll and payroll taxes.

iii. Notes Payable (N/P): Notes payable are obligations in the form of promissory notes with short-term maturity dates of less than 12 months. Often, they are payable upon demand. Otherwise, they have specific maturity dates (typically 30, 60, 90, 180, 270, 360 days maturities). Notes payable include only the principal amount of the debt. Any interest owed is listed under accruals. The proceeds of notes payable should be used to finance current assets (inventory and receivables). The use of funds must be short-term in order for the asset to mature into cash prior to the obligation's maturation. Proper matching would indicate borrowing for seasonal swings in sales, which cause shifts in inventory and receivables, or repaying accounts payable when attractive discount terms are offered for early payment.

    iv. Current portion of Long-Term Debt (LTD)

        1. Proper matching of sources and uses of funds requires that short-term (current) liabilities must be used only to purchase short-term assets (inventory and receivables).

    v. Non-current liabilities obligations that will be payable in the following year. There are three types of non-current liabilities, only two of which are listed on the balance sheet:

        1. Non-current portion of Long-Term Debt (LTD)

2. Notes Payable to Officers, Shareholders, or Owners

3. Contingent Liabilities

vi. Non-current portion of Long-Term Debt (LTD): Non-current portion of LTD is the portion of a term loan that is not due within the next 12 months. It is listed below the current liability section to demonstrate that the loan does not have to be fully liquidated in the coming year. LTD provides cash to be used for a long-term asset purchase, either permanent working capital or fixed assets.

vii. Notes Payable to Officers, Shareholder or Owners: Notes payable to officers, shareholders or owners represent cash that the shareholders or owners must put into the business. For tax reasons, owners may increase their investment beyond the initial business capitalization by making loans to the business rather than purchasing additional stock. Any return on investment to the owners can therefore be paid as a tax-deductible interest expense rather than as non-deductible dividends. When a business borrows from a financial institution, it is common for the officer loans to be subordinated or put on standby. The subordination agreement prohibits the officer from collecting his or her loan prior to the repayment of the institution's loan. When on standby, the loan will be considered as equity by the financial institution.

viii. Contingent Liabilities: Contingent liabilities are potential liabilities not listed on the balance sheet. These are listed in the footnotes because they may never become due and payable. Contingent liabilities may include lawsuits.

If the business has been sued, but the litigation has not been initiated, there is no way of knowing whether the suit will result in a liability. It will be listed in the footnotes because, while not a real liability, it does represent a potential liability that may impair the ability of the business to meet future obligations. Alternatively, if the business guarantees a loan made by a third party to an affiliate, the liability is contingent because it will never become due as long as the affiliate remains healthy and meets its obligations.

8. **Total Liabilities:** Total liabilities represent the sum of all monetary obligations of a business and claims creditors have on its assets.

9. **Equity:** Equity is represented by total assets minus total liabilities. Equity or Net Worth is the most patient and last to mature source of funds. It represents the owners' share in the financing of all the assets.

10. **Income Statement:** The income statement, also known as the profit and loss statement, includes all income and expense accounts over a period of time. This financial statement shows how much money the business will make after all expenses are accounted for. An income statement does not reveal hidden problems, such as insufficient cash flow. Income statements are read from top to bottom.

By this time, you should have a sketch of the financial picture of your business. Now that you have captured that information, you can use it to figure the number sales you need to cover your costs. This is known as the breakeven point. By now you have calculated your fixed costs that consist of lease or rent, monthly payments on your loans, your salary, insurance, or property taxes. Say those fixed costs add up to $6,000, and your product is a necklace. The variable costs associated with producing the necklace are raw material and labor. Variable costs have been calculated to be $0.80 per unit and your necklaces are priced at $2.00 each.

Given this information, we can calculate the breakeven point for the necklace, using the formula below:

$$\$6{,}000 \div (\$2.00 - \$0.80) = 5{,}000 \text{ units}$$

This answer means your business must produce and sell 5,000 necklaces in order to cover your total expenses, fixed and variable. At this level of sales, you will make no profit but will break even.

Let's say you find a way to cut overhead or fixed costs by reducing your own salary by $1,000. That drops your fixed costs from $6,000 to $5,000. Using the same formula and holding all other variables the same, the breakeven point would be:

$$\$5,000 \div (\$2.00-\$0.80) = 4,167 \text{ units}$$

Here, you can see how cutting your fixed costs drops your breakeven point. On the other hand, if you reduce your variable costs by cutting your costs of goods sold to $0.60 per unit and hold other variables the same, then your breakeven point becomes:

$$\$6,000 \div (\$2.00-\$0.60) = 4,286 \text{ units}$$

Now you can reduce your costs and lower your breakeven point without raising your price. If you can reduce your costs and profitably price your products below your competitors' costs, then you can capture more of the market. Your competitors will struggle to compete with your prices and can eventually be driven out of business. As the owner of a home-based business, any decision you make about pricing your product, the costs you incur in your business, and sales volume are interrelated. Calculating the breakeven point is one of the things you need to do before you open for business, and also an essential first step to figure how much product you need to sell to make a profit.

Based on my market analysis, I can charge _____ for my product or service.

My monthly fixed costs total

_____

____.

My variable cost per unit

is_____.

I need to sell

_____units to

breakeven.

Chapter 11:

The Home-Based Business Accelerator

Cash is like water on your seedling business; you need it to grow. The Home-Based Business Accelerator is the injection of cash you will use to get your venture off the ground. This chapter will examine the things investors look for when evaluating a company for an injection of the cash to ramp up your business. The money can come to you in two ways: in the form of a loan, or in the form of equity. You must pay back a loan, but you do not repay equity like you would repay a loan; instead, you are exchanging a percentage of ownership in your company for the cash you need. This section talks about the latter form, equity. You should keep these concepts in mind as you develop your business plan.

After Michael Roberts and Lauren Barley interviewed Russell Siegelman, a venture capitalist at KPCB, they published a number of key things that investors examine before they fund a company. Below are some of their insights[22]:

1. **Large market opportunity in a fast-growing sector.** If you are looking for a $100,000 investment to start your business, you need to demonstrate that the market is large and it is growing. You may need to provide evidence to support the market size being $10,000,000 or larger for that investment. Be prepared to provide research to back that up, along with projections about the 5-year outlook on the market growth rate.

2. **Sustainable competitive advantage.** What can your business do more effectively than your competition? Can you prove that you can do it better for at least two to three more years before they can catch up? Does your business solve a tough problem that has not been solved before?

---

[22] Roberts, M. J.

3. **An outstanding team**. Who are your team members and what is their experience? If your business is just you, explain how your unique experience makes you highly qualified to operate a profitable business. What is your track record on projects you have managed? Investors want to know about successful projects you led in the past and for you to support your story with data such as sales reports and tax returns.
4. **Your business model.** Is your product or service well understood, or is it a new technology? Are you an online retailer like Amazon with an enormous cost advantage and a high volume of sales? Or did you just create a new mobile application that will appeal to millions of users? Be prepared to explain your value proposition in great detail, as well as how you get customers and how much it costs to acquire a new customer.
5. **Your timing.** Are you an early entrant into this market? How many other businesses are doing what you are

doing? What are their sales? How long have they been in business?

6. **Your customers.** Who is your customer? What does (s)he look like? How old? Where does your customer live and work? Is your customer influential online? In other words, when prospective customers see your influential customer, do they want to buy things because (s)he has them?

7. **Your industry.** Have you connected with an expert in your industry? If an investor were to call someone in your industry and ask that person about your business model, what would that person say?

8. **References.** If you are seeking a sizable investment, the investors may contact your references and some blind references. They will ask others how effectively you execute your strategies, how well you follow through on your commitments, and a validation of your capabilities.

9. **Patience.** It can take six weeks or more before you get a deal, so be willing to wait.

10. **Financial statements.** Most of the time, your financial projections will be too low or too high when you are getting started. Ideally, you would exceed your projections. Many investors look at your financials as a test of your credibility. Are they reasonable and consistent with operational needs of the business? If you claim your costs are low and your profits are high, that needs to be reflected in your financials. A credible entrepreneur knows how to explain the technical side of the business and justify the numbers behind it.

The total size of my market is $_____, and I know this because _____.

The market is growing at a rate of _____%, and I know this because

_____

_____

_____.

The three major competitors in this market are

_____,

_____, and

_____.

If there are "no competitors," three of the things customers would spend money on instead of my product or service are

_____,

_____, and

_____.

The things my business can do more effectively than my competitors are

_____

_____

_____

_____

_____.

Chapter 12:

Obtaining Startup Funding

At some point, you will discover that starting a business without funding is very difficult. Your own resources can only carry you so far, and once you add up all the costs associated with launching your business, you will probably need some support to get going. If your product has a development cycle that requires special equipment—or even if it takes you time to make things by hand—you will need cash to pay your expenses between sales. This is due to the lag that naturally occurs between the money you spend to get something and the time it takes to receive the money you get from selling it. It can often take a year or more before the business can stand on its own cash flow, and even longer before your business generates enough revenue to pay yourself a salary equivalent to a regular full-time salary. This chapter is about obtaining the funding you need to get started and to sustain your business while it grows.

You can get the funding you need to start your business from many different sources. Maybe you are considering cashing in your 401(k) or IRA retirement savings, or asking a friend or family member to be an investor in your venture. There are inherent risks in those choices, for your business always runs the possibility of failure, and you need to weigh your decision carefully before tapping those resources. For example, would your relationship with that friend or family member be ruined if the business went bankrupt? How many more years could you work at a regular job to recover the savings you used to start the business if it failed? Given the complex nature of the human relations involved in obtaining these sources of funding, it may be advantageous to study the most common ways to get the money you need to get going: crowdfunding, venture capital, and commercial banks.

Crowdfunding is a method of raising capital through the collective effort of friends, family, customers, and individual investors. This approach taps into the collective efforts of a large pool of individuals—primarily online via social media and crowdfunding platforms—and leverages their networks for greater reach and exposure[23]. Websites like GoFundMe and Kickstarter are leaders in this space, providing hundreds of millions in capital for businesses like yours.

---

[23] "What is Crowdfunding?"

The way crowdfunding works is basically the opposite of the old-fashioned method of getting an investment in your company. Historically, people raised money by taking a business plan, market research, and prototypes to a few wealthy investment banks or investors. People would need to go to banks, angel investors, or venture capital firms, which did not give many options. Obtaining funding can be very difficult because you usually need to provide a track-record of your business success, and you may be required to attend meetings away from your business during business hours.

Crowdfunding platforms, unlike banks and other firms, give you the flexibility to publish your business idea along with your offerings for investors to view and support online. You save money because you are not travelling to sell your idea, and you save time that you can devote to advancing your business. With crowdfunding, it is much easier to get your opportunity in front of more interested parties and give them more ways to help grow your business. From investing thousands of dollars in exchange for a percentage of ownership to as little as a few dollars in exchange for a pre-order on a new product before it hits the market.

When you make a campaign, you should include a powerful reason behind the idea, exciting and unique benefits for participating, and an eye-catching display. Including a demonstration video is a must. It helps to show investors what your product does, and this also enables them to see the face—and hear the story—behind the company. The story should be compelling to watch because many consumers will tune out if they do not connect to the video, as this is really the gateway to your proposal. You must also deliver what you promise.

Obtaining venture capital is like being on the TV series *Shark Tank*. You take your business plan to an individual or panel of investors, and convince them to provide you with financing in exchange for partial company ownership. There is always a give and take; you must give the investors something in exchange for the cash they provide. This process can occur in several stages: seed, early stage, later stage, and bridge.

The first stage of venture capital financing is called the seed-stage. This stage of funding is relatively small, and is used to finance the early development of a new product or service. The money is usually directed toward product development, market research, building a management team, and developing a business plan. A genuine seed-stage company usually has not yet started generating cash flow from sales; therefore the money invested is used to get the business to the point where it can start generating cash from operations. It is very difficult to get financing at this stage from institutional investors, so you may need to go to your personal network or crowdfunding sources to get past this point. An initial seed investment round from a professional VC firm typically ranges from $250,000 to $1 million[24], if you are fortunate to receive one. The VC fund that provides seed funding is also likely to participate in later funding rounds with other partners to finance equipment, sales, distribution, inventory, and parts.

The next stage is called early stage. This is for companies

---

[24] "The Stages in Venture Capital Investing"

that are able to begin operations but are not yet at the stage of commercial manufacturing and sales. This early stage financing supports increased capabilities for the business to expand. New businesses can consume large amounts of money and costs can easily spiral out of control, therefore controls need to be in place to mitigate risks during this stage.

The startup process occurs during the early stage, and is when product and marketing campaigns begin. Startup financing provides funds to companies for product development and initial marketing. This type of financing is usually provided to new companies that have organized under a form of business ownership such as an LLC or corporation, or to those that have been in business for a short time, but have not yet sold their product in the marketplace. Generally, such firms have already assembled key management, prepared a business plan, and conducted market studies. During this stage, the business also realizes its first revenues but has yet to show a profit. This is often where the enterprise brings in its first "outside" investors. If you are familiar with *Shark Tank*, this is the stage of funding for many of the contestants.

During the "first stage" described above, cash is provided to initiate commercial manufacturing and sales. Most first stage companies have been in business less than three years and have a product or service in testing or pilot production. In some cases, the product may be commercially available, and the company may be generating revenue.

During the later stage, capital is provided after commercial manufacturing and sales but before any initial public offering. The product or service is in production and is commercially available. The company demonstrates significant revenue growth, but may or may not be showing a profit. It has usually been in business for more than three years.

After establishing a track record of revenue growth, the business may be ready to bridge over to an initial public offering. This is commonly referred to as "going public," and the time when the owners and investors generally receive a substantial return on the equity they hold in the company. When your business goes public, anyone can own a percentage of it as long as he or she can afford the stock. As of 2016, your business will need to be generating at least $1,000,000 per year in income and valued at least $8,000,000 to "go public" and be listed on the NASDAQ exchange.

Here are some suggestions to save money when you get started, so the dollars you receive can go even further:

- Buy used instead of new equipment
- Lease equipment instead of buying it
- Obtain payments from customers in advance when possible
- Search for things you need on eBay, rather than at full-price stores

- Hire interns
- Buy recycled printer cartridges
- If you use credit cards, shop for lower interest rates and rewards programs, and avoid cash advances
- Form a buying alliance by joining a business or a trade association for bulk purchasing discounts
- Be reluctant to extend credit to new customers unless you know their credit history
- Resolve complaints before they escalate into legal matters
- Negotiate payment terms with your suppliers to receive discounts if you pay early

I plan on starting my business using funds from

_____

_____

_____.

I have visited the following crowdfunding sites

_____

_____

_____.

Other businesses similar to mine have received crowdfunding in the amount of $

_____

_____

_____.

In exchange for $20 of funding, my business is willing to provide

_____

_____.

For $100 in funding, it will provide

_____

_____.

For $250 in funding, it will provide

_____

_____.

For $1,000 in funding, it will provide

_____

_____.

If an investor asked me what I need the money for, I would say

_____

_____

_____

_____

_____.

Chapter 13:
Creating a Proposal for a Prospective Customer

Your home-based business can take many forms, but regardless of which form you choose, you need to convince customers to use your product or service. One way to do that is through a business proposal. It is your company's offer to complete a specific job or project, to supply a service, or be the vendor of a certain product. It is generally a document sent to a prospective client that outlines the service(s) offered, and explains why you are the best person for the job. The proposal is sometimes a very thorough, detailed estimate.

Writing business proposals involves a lot of upfront work. Once you become aware of a potential client seeking proposals in your business niche, you can develop a sound, clear, and precise business proposal. There are many pre-planning activities you will want to conduct[25].

You will start by researching your customer and the problem you can solve for him/her. If you are targeting a business client, check the company website. There you may find names of the people who could potentially approve your proposal. You can also get an idea of the business model, how long it been in business, its goals, and its financial picture. It would be ideal to arrange a meeting with management before you write the proposal. You may not meet the CEO, but you should make an appointment with the highest-level manager. During that meeting, you want the prospective customer to clarify goals and needs, and take detailed notes of that information. Get clear budget parameters to have a financial framework for your proposal. While the focus of this meeting must be on the client,

---

[25] Priesler, A.

include examples of your successes with similar organizations/industries to showcase the ways you can help this customer specifically.

Once you understand the customer's goals and needs, make a plan to solve them as efficiently as possible. For example, if you are in the property management business, and you become aware that a large apartment complex owner is looking for a new outside property management firm, you should meet with that owner or his representative. Ask about his issues and problems, as well as what made him unhappy with the previous management. These will be critical points in your solution proposal.

- The greatest challenge facing this industry is

_____

_____

_____.

- The current challenge this customer is facing is

_____

_____

_____.

- The customer determined this problem existed by

_____

_____

_____.

- In the past, the customer addressed this issue by

_____

_____

_____.

- The customer's other areas of need affected by this proposal are

_____

_____

_____.

- The customer's desired outcome is

_____

_____

_____.

- The customer wants this finished by

_____

_____

_____.

- My customer's budget for this is

_____

_____

_____.

You will occasionally be asked to provide a proposal (or estimate), and sometimes not, but supply one anyway. When a prospective client asks for a proposal, it is called *solicited*, but when you are not asked, it is called *unsolicited*. The only difference is whether the customer asks you to provide one. However, if a customer asks for a proposal, (s)he is more likely to have decided to make a purchase and is now evaluating different vendors.

With a solicited proposal, your prospective client may issue an RFP, or "request for proposal." This is exactly what it sounds like—they want you to send over a business proposal for review. A proposal is very different than a business plan; so let's take a look at how it differs. Although it is a separate document, your proposal may include some information the business plan contains.

In the proposal, you are attempting to sell your prospective client on your product or service, not on your business itself. You are not seeking funding, as you are with a business plan.

You are seeking to gain a new customer.

I want to make clear that a business proposal is not just an estimate; although you will likely touch on costs and outline these details in your business proposal, an estimate is much more informal and only takes a quick look at the costs, not the whole picture.

A proposal needs to address three basic ideas, "The Three P's". As you write your proposal, keep these elements in mind: problem statement, proposed solution, and pricing.

The problem statement comes after the title page, table of contents, and executive summary. Your business proposal should start with a title page, which includes your name, your company name, the name of the person to whom you are submitting your proposal, and the date submitted. Depending on your business proposal length, a table of contents will help the customer navigate it efficiently. Include it after your title page, and before you reveal the finer details of the proposal. Introduce it with a succinct executive summary—one that really sells your business and what it has to offer.

If you have written a business plan, you can use some of its content in this section, too.

Following your executive summary, discuss the problem that the client needs your company's help to solve. Think of "problem" or "issue" in very general terms because their main problem may just be finding the right person to complete a project. This is your opportunity to show new customers that you understand their needs, and fully grasp the issue they are trying to solve. Show them that you understand what they need by summarizing the issue they are facing in your own words.

It is helpful to include an approach and methodology section to show your plan on tackling your potential client's problem, and the steps you will take to carry out your plan. This is where you will get into the details of how you actually plan to give the customer what he/she needs. While earlier proposal sections may have been generalized, this detailed section of the business proposal includes what steps you will take to solve their problem. Be cautious of going into too much detail because the customer may be overwhelmed and overlook some information. The goal is for the customer to get a clear sense of the actual proposal.

You should also include a qualifications section to convince your potential client why you are the most qualified person to take on the job. You can mention any relevant education, industry specific training or certifications, past successful projects of a similar nature, years of experience, and so on.

Next, you want to include your schedule and benchmarks. Tell the customer what you will do, and when it will be finished. Ensure you and your prospective client are in agreement from the beginning about the project scope and sequence so the relationship stays positive. This will help you to not set your client up with unrealistic expectations. While you might be tempted to underestimate how long it will take you to complete the project, refrain from doing so. Do not promise what you cannot deliver! If you are offering a product, this section might not be applicable to you, so feel free to remove it.

Outlining the cost, payment terms, and any legal matters are important, too. You may need to establish a payment schedule if it is a large project divided into phases, and progress payments are due on completion of each phase. The way you structure this section will largely depend on the particular project or service you are offering. A section entitled "Fee Summary" may be sufficient if a one-time payment is required; otherwise, a "Fee Schedule" list might be more appropriate. Always consult the customer's RFP whenever possible to ensure you are supplying all the information they need to help make a decision.

If there are any legal issues to attend to, such as permits or licensing, include this information here. You can add a section entirely devoted to handling the legal side of the project, if need be.

The benefits section is where you can highlight your service in terms of the value it will create for the customer. Tell the customer everything (s)he will gain from using your service. For example, you can explain why you are the best choice, and all the ways in which their business will benefit from choosing you and your business as their solution. Here are some prompts to help you write the benefits section:

- When working with a similar company, or on a similar problem, my solution was

  _____

_____
_____.

- As a result of my solution, the customer was able to

_____

_____
_____.

- I can do a better job than my competition because

_____

_____
_____.

- Who will do the work

_____
_____.

- Who will manage the work

  _____

  _____.

- Who does the customer call if there is a problem

  _____

  _____.

- Who is responsible for what needs to be done/delivered, what will be required to do it, what can the customer expect, and what will it cost

  _____

  _____

  _____.

- Where will the work be done and where will it be delivered

  _____

_____
_____.

- How will work be done to achieve quality assurance and customer satisfaction

_____
_____
_____.

- How will risks be reduced

_____
_____
_____.

- When will you start

_____
_____.

- When will key milestones be scheduled

  _____

  _____

  _____.

- When will the project be complete

  _____

  _____.

- When is payment due

  _____

  _____.

Below is a sample proposal for an event planning service business for your reference. You can find many templates on websites such as Pandadoc, which has a wealth of professional templates that you can use to get started. You will need to adapt some sections of this proposal to match your business.

The Importance of Hiring a Professional Event Management Partner - **Introduction**

In-person events are a great way to give people the right impression of your company. These types of events offer a look into the company's culture, showing you the corporation's nuts and bolts. An effective event can build your reputation with customers, prospective customers, media, and other important people. But a flawed event can damage your company's reputation.

For that reason, you should take time to research the right management company to coordinate your events. You need experts who can: (1) plan the whole event, (2) coordinate all the tasks required to deliver a quality event, (3) manage your vendors, be reliable, and reply promptly when you need support, and (4) measure event outcomes and returns on the money you spend.

As your event management partner, [***Your Company Name***] will help oversee every step of the event planning and execution process. Let us manage your labor-intensive event logistics so you can stay focused on more strategic activities.

Who We Are

We are a professional, creative team of event management specialists with [# OF YEARS] years of experience producing great events of any type. We are detail-oriented and passionate about running events so our clients don't need to worry about them. Our goal is to represent you by providing you and your guests with superior event experiences. Our objective is to exceed your expectations and business requirements, our valued customer, by helping you host great events.

Our Understanding of Your Needs

We have reviewed your initial requirements and understand the following key facts about your event:

Event Name:

Date(s):

Location:

Projected Number of Attendees:

Every event is unique and special. Each has its own distinct audience, tone, personality, and set of business objectives. In the beginning, [***Company Name***] will meet with you to understand your goals for the event. We will then set up a strategy and execution plan accordingly. [***Company Name***] focuses on improving processes and coordinating people so that your event's best qualities shine through and it runs smoothly.

We will work with you to clarify your targeted business outcomes for your event. In our experience, typical strategic goals for similar corporate events include:

- Reinforcing brand identity and key messages
- Positioning the host organization as an industry thought leader
- Educating attendees on products and/or services
- Interacting with customers, prospects and other company constituents
- Identifying and advancing sales leads
- Generating media coverage for the sponsoring company
- Providing inspiring and engaging content for the audience

We align our proven practices to address your needs in every step of the process. That way, we ensure your desired outcomes stay at the forefront of every decision.

What We Do for You

We will manage the whole process of your event so you can focus on larger business strategies. For a full list of services, see the Pricing section below.

To make sure your event receives the right amount of attendees, we will assign a dedicated project manager to your event. We will hold weekly planning and budget reviews to ensure costs and tasks are within your budget, and we will be accountable to meet your deadlines.

Total Cost

Our proposed pricing for end-to-end management of your event is [$$$]. Payments will be split into a non-refundable retainer—due at project initiation—along with interim payments and a final payment as described in the enclosed Event Management Agreement. The pricing table below contains a detailed cost breakdown for each of our key areas of responsibility.

[Create and insert your pricing table to itemize the costs]

Letter of Agreement

This agreement is between [Client's Company Name], hereafter referred to as CLIENT, and [Company Name], hereafter referred to as CONTRACTOR.

Description of Services

CONTRACTOR will provide event logistic management services, as detailed in the letter proposal dated [Proposal Date] for CLIENT's [Event Name] on [Date of Event].

Pricing and Payment Terms

The total cost of event management services provided by the CONTRACTOR is [$$$]. CLIENT will make payments as follows:

- A non-refundable retainer in the amount of [$$$] upon acceptance of this agreement.
- [$$$] due on Date (deadline date in which this agreement is valid)
- [$$$] due on Date (ten days prior to your event)

- [$$$] due on Date (thirty days after your event)

Term and Termination

This agreement will terminate automatically upon completion of the services required by this letter of agreement.

Changes and Cancellations

Any and all changes made to this letter of agreement must be made in writing and signed by all parties. If the event is cancelled, refunds are limited to unearned fees, funds in excess of unused or non-refundable fees, and out-of-pocket expenses. If CLIENT cancels less than [#] of days before the event, there will be no refund issued.

Now that you have an overview of a business proposal and an example of the structure, it is time to get some experience writing one. I suggest that you create a template in advance of transacting business; have someone review it and check for any gaps in coverage or areas that may be unclear. Your aim is to avoid future disputes that can cost your business time and money to resolve.

Chapter 14:

Patents, Trademarks, and Protecting Your Intellectual Property

When you start a new business, you may feel hesitant to share your business idea with others out of fear that they will "steal" it. In some cases, you may need to keep it top secret, but most of the time, you need to get your ideas out and start testing the waters. Before you do that, however, you need to understand intellectual property, patents, trademarks, copyrights, and trade secrets.

By virtue of the fact that you want to operate a home-based business, you probably possess some knowledge, information, or ideas that will be essential for your success. In fact, your intellectual property might be your most valuable asset, especially if you have a publishing business model. Intellectual property is a global term that is any product of human intellect that is intangible but has value in the marketplace. It can be the result of your creativity or imagination. Ideas are the currency of the information age, and unlike gold, their value is difficult to estimate. Therefore, you need to build your own bank for ideas to keep them safe. Some common mistakes made in this space are not properly identifying all of your intellectual property, not recognizing its full value, not using it as part of the business plan, or not properly identifying all of it.

Your starting point needs to be identifying what to protect. Here are some exercises you can use to determine what you need to protect:

- The things that give my company an advantage over other companies are

  _____

  _____

  _____

  _____

  _____.

- The value of my ideas in the marketplace is

  _____

  _____

  _____

  _____

  _____.

In other words, you need to determine if the intellectual property gives your company an advantage AND has value in the marketplace. Some entrepreneurs are not successful because they go through the time and expense of patenting something unsellable because it holds no customer value. You need to put a price on it, and in some cases, be prepared to pay legal fees to defend your patent in court. Unlike a case of theft of physical property, such as buildings and equipment, you cannot call 911 and have the police department to send out all available units to apprehend someone copying your ideas. However, there is a website called www.stopfakes.gov that provides information about how to file a complaint if you believe someone has copied your product and is infringing on your intellectual property.

One of the ways to protect your property, and one you may be most familiar with, is the patent. It is essentially the right to exclude others from making, selling, or using an invention for a period of time. Note that this is the right, not the obligation, which means you can choose who gets access to it. However, you also have to police it; the government will not do that for you. This can become messy for your business if your patented object is built from components that are patented by someone else. If that is the case, you will need to obtain permission from the other party to use those components in your product. Sometimes permission is given in exchange for a licensing fee, where your company pays a percentage of the revenue to the other party for the rights to use its components in your product.

The philosophy behind the patent is to give you and your investors protection for a period of time to recover your costs of designing, manufacturing, and selling something. Neither investors nor inventors would have much incentive to develop something new if they could not recover their costs for making it. Who would want to go into business to see how much money they can lose? It sounds absurd, but without some protections, that could be reality. It can take two to three years for the United States Patent and Trademark Office (USPTO) to grant you a patent, so it would be advantageous for you to start early. If you cannot wait that long and want to test the product in the market, you can obtain a provisional patent relatively quickly, which will provide you with a limited amount of protection while you test your invention's traction in the marketplace. For additional details, visit the USPTO at www.uspto.gov.

The prices for patents range from $5,000 to $15,000+ depending on the complexity of the invention. Depending on the size of your organization and the type of patent, it costs approximately $700 to file, plus an additional ~$500 when it is issued, and then maintenance fees ranging from $800 to $3,700 (depending on the age of the patent). On top of that, you have attorney fees which can add up quickly if you have a complex technology or something that is Internet-based, such as a social media system. Then you may need to wait two to three years to find out if the patent has been granted. If you are in a high-tech field, your invention may be obsolete in three years.

Trademarks are another commonly used method to protect intellectual property. A trademark is any word, name, symbol, or device used to identify the source/origin of products or services, and distinguishes them from others. The Nike brand illustrates the importance of a trademark. How would that brand be impacted if every shoe manufacturer in the country could put a Nike swoosh on any pair of shoes it wanted? The real Nike would suffer tremendous financial losses. The trademark protects the brand from other companies using it without permission.

If you want to apply for a trademark, you will need to decide if you want it to be a service mark, which will identify services or business activities rather than actual products. You can think of this as protecting the name of the service you provide so competitors cannot use your name. You could also use a certification mark to verify that the product or service has a specific quality, such as certified organic by [your company name]. The other form of mark you could use is called a collective mark, which indicates membership in a trade association such as the American Medical Association (AMA).

Once you have selected the appropriate mark, you may be ready to apply at the USPTO. It is usually best to pick something that is distinct and visually appealing. After you select your prospective trademark, you need to conduct a search to see if anyone else is using it. You can do this search yourself, or hire an attorney, which is helpful but not necessary. Visit the USPTO website and conduct the trademark search on the federal and state level for the state where you want to do business. It pays to be thorough in this search because if your mark is challenged, and you lose, you may need to destroy everything you put that symbol on.

Your last step is creating rights in the trademark. If your symbol is very distinctive, and you are the first one to use it, you are the owner. This is just the beginning, not the end, of the process. The trademark must then go through a period of secondary meaning, when customers begin to identify your trademark with a specific product—your product. Kleenex is a perfect example, where people generally refer to all facial tissues as Kleenex. This happened with Xerox and copy machines, and Coke with soft drinks. The USPTO can start to offer protection once you file an intent-to-use trademark application. Once you file that application, you receive the benefits of registering. It will cost $200 - $300 to file, and can take close to one year to get the trademark registered.

Your other option for protecting your property is by a copyright. It is a form of protection provided by the laws of the United States for "original works of authorship", including literary, dramatic, musical, architectural, cartographic, choreographic, pantomimic, pictorial, graphic, sculptural, and audiovisual creations. "Copyright" literally means the right to copy but has evolved to mean the body of exclusive rights granted by law to copyright owners for protection of their work. Copyright protection does not extend to any idea, procedure, process, system, title, principle, or discovery[26]. Similarly, names, titles, short phrases, slogans, familiar symbols, mere variations of typographic ornamentation, lettering, coloring, and listings of contents or ingredients are not subject to copyright. There are copyright laws that state when you put an original work in written form, it is automatically protected.

---

[26] "U.S. Copyright Office Definitions"

Here are examples of things you can copyright: books, poetry, blogs, reference works, speeches, advertising, games, computer programs, apps, etc. The rule of thumb is that if the work has been recorded, it can be copyrighted. As nice as it may be if they could be copyrighted, ideas are not eligible for copyright protection. In other words, if you want to open a hockey-themed restaurant, that idea cannot be protected. However, if you made blueprints and recorded the design, then you could copyright the expression of that idea. While we are on the topic of restaurants, it is important to note that recipes cannot be copyrighted.

Although you cannot copyright certain things, such as secret formulas that are critical to your success, they are still your trade secrets. This information can be just as valuable to your organization as the trademark. The subject matter of trade secrets is usually defined in broad terms and includes sales methods, distribution methods, consumer profiles, advertising strategies, lists of suppliers and clients, and manufacturing processes. While a final determination of what information constitutes a trade secret will depend on the circumstances of each individual case, clearly unfair practices of secret information include: industrial or commercial espionage, breach of contract, and breach of confidence.

Unlike patents, trade secrets are protected without registration, that is, trade secrets are protected without any procedural formalities. Consequently, a trade secret can be protected for an unlimited period of time[27]. Here are six factors[28] to consider when determining whether information constitutes a trade secret:

- The extent to which the information is known outside the claimant's business
- The extent to which it is known by employees and others involved in the business
- The extent of measures taken by the claimant to guard the secrecy of the information
- The value of the information to the business and its competitors
- The amount of effort or money expended by the business in developing the information

---

[27] "How are Trade Secrets Protected?"
[28] "Trade secret"

- The ease or difficulty with which the information could be properly acquired or duplicated by others

If you think you have reason to file a claim against someone who may have taken your trade secret, there are three essential elements to consider:

- The subject matter involved must qualify for trade secret protection; it must be the type of information trade secret was intended to protect, and it must not be generally known.
- The holder of the trade secret must establish that reasonable precautions were taken to prevent disclosure of the secret information.
- The trade secret holder must prove that the information was wrongfully acquired, and that the information was misappropriated.

Just because another organization uses a trade secret belonging to another, it does not always constitute misappropriation. There are two basic situations in which obtaining the use of a trade secret is illegal: where it is acquired through improper means or where it involves a breach of confidence[29]. Trade secrets may be obtained by lawful means such as independent discovery, reverse engineering, and inadvertent disclosure resulting from the trade secret holder's failure to take reasonable protective measures.

---

[29] "Trade secret"

Protective measures can be physical or written agreements. You can protect trade secrets by restricting access to the employees who have a genuine need to know them. This may only be one chemist in your laboratory, for example. You can also label documents as "confidential" to indicate restricted access. Protecting things with passwords is also an effective method of protecting information from unauthorized use. If you are concerned about employees sharing trade secrets, it is important to inform employees about your policies, and ask them to sign non-disclosure and non-compete agreements.

Once you are underway, it is vital to periodically take inventory of your intellectual property. Keep records of the dates and times you create things. If they are your ideas, note that. If they are developed in collaboration, document when the collaboration occurred and the responsible parties. Your goal is to have a list of the things that belong to your organization and when they were created, just in case you need to refer back to them should a dispute arise.

Chapter 15:

The End Game

What do you want from your business? Do you want to keep this business in your home forever? Would you like to open a storefront? You may have many reasons for starting your business, and as awkward as it may seem to talk about reasons for exiting your business, it is important to plan the beginning with the end in mind.

Your business plan should include a section dedicated to stating your intentions. For example, if you are seeking startup capital, you need to explain to your investors how they will recover the money they invested. Perhaps you want to establish this as a family business to pass down to the next generation, in which case, you need to have that plan in place. If that is your goal, make sure you have buy-back agreements with your investors that will enable you to repurchase some of the ownership at a later time if you choose to do so.

One popular strategy is growth through licensing and franchising. Licensing is basically renting your brand, or other intellectual property, to increase sales. Let's say you develop a popular mobile phone case (like an Otterbox) that you can make up to a maximum quantity within your own capabilities, and a retailer like AT&T thinks it would be great to put that logo directly on the phone. AT&T then makes a deal to put your logo directly on the back of phones to make them seem more durable in the eyes of the consumer, and gives your company a percentage of the sales.

Licensing can be effective when you have a strong belief that your company's brand will improve as a result of the licensing deal. Your brand would probably benefit greatly by appearing in AT&T stores and on its website. However, you cannot always control every aspect of the value chain for your product. For example, if your logo appears on a t-shirt that has obscenity written on the back, it might harm your brand. You need to screen prospective licensing deals carefully and put mechanisms in place to protect your brand, which can take you years to build and moments to ruin.

You may be wondering when is the right time to exit a business? In most industries, you can expect to spend at least ten years scaling up your business to the point where it is large enough to sell it, take it public, or merge with another company. You will probably exit from the management team and become an investor, providing consulting services to your company for a period of time during the transition. It may seem like a trivial point to you as the entrepreneur, but this is very important to your investors, who will want to know upfront how they will convert their investment into cash or stock in the future.

So let's say you're at the point where you are ready to sell the business. How do you calculate the value? Like anything else that can be bought or sold, its value is whatever someone else will pay for it and what you are willing to accept. You probably have an intuitive understanding of the valuation already. For example, is a business that is losing money worth less than a business that is making money? With everything else being equal, yes, it is. Why? Because a buyer will buy your company because (s)he believes that it will be more valuable in the future than it is today. Positive cash flow is one way to demonstrate that the business is worthwhile.

How about a business that has many assets, such as equipment, land, and buildings? These are known as the book value of the business. It is the value that remains when the liabilities are subtracted from the assets. Businesses that have large book values are worth more than those with smaller book values, everything else being equal.

Regardless of how the business is valued, it is only an estimate. The true value is what someone finally pays for it.

To maximize the potential price for which you can sell your business, you should reinvest as much profit as you can into the business to make it grow. Then, when you are ready to sell, you can remove money without decreasing sales; and be patient, for it can take some time to secure an offer.

One way to sell a company is through a management buyout. In this strategy, you hire one or more skilled managers who help you operate the business for a period of time and then they buy it from you when you are ready to sell it. You can get the emotional satisfaction of selling it to people you know, and if it is a profitable operation, managers want to buy it.

You could also offer an employee stock ownership plan. Here is your opportunity to establish a plan that allows your employees to buy company stock as part of their retirement. When you are ready to retire, the plan borrows money to buy your stock, and that stock is added back to the plan as the loan is paid off. For example, if the plan has 100 shares of stock altogether and you own 60 shares while the employees own the other 40 shares, the business takes out a loan to buy your 60 shares for cash. Then, as the loan is paid off, the stock is added back to the plan. This would not be a good strategy, however, if you do not want the employees to have control of the company.

Merging or being acquired by another company can be an exit strategy if you want your company to grow by becoming part of another company. This can be very challenging, and negotiations can take over a year to complete. The key principle behind buying a company is to create shareholder value over and above that of the sum of the two companies. Two companies together are more valuable than two separate companies—at least, as that is the reasoning behind the merger.

This rationale is particularly attractive to companies when times are tough. Strong companies will buy other companies to create a more competitive, cost-efficient company. The companies will come together hoping to gain a greater market share or to achieve greater efficiency. Due to these potential benefits, you may be in a position to agree to be purchased when you know you cannot survive alone.

Although they are often used together, the terms merger and acquisition mean slightly different things. For example, when one company takes over another and makes it clear that it is the new owner, the purchase is called an acquisition. Legally, the target company does not exist anymore and the buyer "gobbles up" the business and the buyer's stock continues to be traded.

What is more likely to happen is a merger, when your company and another company, sometimes about the same size, agree to go forward as a single new company rather than remain separately owned and operated. This kind of action is more precisely referred to as a "merger of equals." Both companies' stocks are surrendered and new company stock is issued in its place. For example, both Daimler-Benz and Chrysler ceased to exist when the two firms merged, and a new company, DaimlerChrysler, was created.

In practice, however, mergers of equals do not happen very often. Usually, one company will buy another and they agree to allow the acquired firm to proclaim that the action is a merger of equals, even if it was really an acquisition. Being bought out is often seen as a negative thing, so by calling the deal a "merger," deal makers and top managers make the takeover more pleasant[30].

A purchase deal will also be called a merger when both CEOs agree that joining together is in the best interest of both of their companies. However, when the deal is unfriendly—that is, when the target company does not want to be purchased—It is regarded as an acquisition, and sometimes referred to as a hostile takeover.

Whether a purchase is considered a merger or an acquisition depends on whether the purchase is friendly or hostile and how it is announced. In other words, the real difference lies in how the purchase is communicated and received by the target company's board of directors, employees, and shareholders.

Besides doing this to exit the business, you use a merger to create synergy. This is the magic force that allows for new advantages for the new business. Synergy takes the form of revenue enhancement and cost savings. By merging, your company and the buyer aim to benefit from the following:

---

[30] McClure, B.

Staff reductions - your employees may be aware that a merger could lead to job losses. Consider all the money that is saved from reducing the number of staff members from accounting, marketing and other departments. Job cuts will also include the former CEO; in this case, it will probably be you, who typically leaves with a generous compensation package.

Economies of scale - Bigger can be better. Whether you are buying stationary or a new corporate IT system, a bigger company placing the orders can save more on costs. Mergers also translate into improved purchasing power to buy equipment or office supplies - when placing larger orders, companies have a greater ability to negotiate prices with suppliers.

Acquiring new technology - To stay competitive, companies need to keep up with technological developments and their business applications. By buying a smaller company with unique technology, a large company can maintain or develop a competitive edge.

Improved market reach and industry visibility -

Companies buy companies to reach new markets, and grow revenues and earnings. A merge may expand two companies' marketing and distribution, giving them new sales opportunities. A merger can also improve a company's standing in the investment community: bigger firms often have an easier time raising capital than smaller ones.

That said, the amount of synergy created is uncertain, and is easier said than done - it is not automatically realized once two companies merge. In theory, there should be some minimum gains when two businesses are combined, but sometimes a merger does just the opposite. In many cases, one and one can add up to less than two.

Whatever your reason for starting, or exiting, your home-based business, you should always remind yourself of your reason for opening shop in the first place, your big WHY. Hopefully, in this journey, you find and do work you love, get paid for doing it, and you can do it so well that you have an advantage over other businesses trying to do the same thing.

Whether you go into it alone, or you bring in your family or investors, remember your reasons for doing this work so that you can tap into those reasons—step on your home-based business accelerator.

References

Applegate, L. (2015, July 17). "Recognizing and Shaping Opportunities." Entrepreneurship: Core Curriculum

Ayu, A. (2016, February 11). "10 Things to Consider When Starting a Family Business" Retrieved September 12, 2016, from http://www.inc.com/ariana-ayu/10-things-to-consider-when-starting-a-family-business.html

Beesley, C. (2016, February 22). Run a Home-Based

Business? – Find the Licenses and Permits You Need | The U.S. Small Business Administration | SBA.gov. Retrieved September 08, 2016, from https://www.sba.gov/blogs/run-home-based-business-find-licenses-and-permits-you-need

Belcher, L. (n.d.). "How to Build an Internet Publishing Business" Retrieved September 16, 2016, from http://smallbusiness.chron.com/build-internet-publishing-business-31277.html

Biery, M. (2015, September 6). "These Industries Generate The Highest Profit Margins" Retrieved August 30, 2016, from http://www.forbes.com/sites/sageworks/2015/09/06/these-industries-generate-the-highest-profit-margins/#7f28b46564ac

Dinsmore, S. (2012, October). How to find work you love. Retrieved August 24, 2016, from https://www.ted.com/talks/scott_dinsmore_how_to_find_work_you_love

Fishkin, R. (2016, July 15). 8 Rules for How to Choose a Domain Name - Whiteboard Friday. Retrieved September 14, 2016, from https://moz.com/blog/how-to-choose-a-domain-name-whiteboard-friday

Gourville, J. T. "Eager Sellers and Stony Buyers: Understanding the Psychology of New-Product Adoption," Harvard Business Review 84 =(June 2006): 99–106

"How are Trade Secrets Protected?" (n.d.). Retrieved September 29, 2016, from http://www.wipo.int/sme/en/ip_business/

trade_secrets/protection.htm

Humphrey, J. (2015). "7 Ways To Enjoy The Process Of Starting Your Own Business." Retrieved August 02, 2016, from http://www.fastcompany.com/3044832/hit-the-ground-running/7-ways-to-enjoy-the-process-of-starting-your-own-business

Landau, C. (2016). "How to Turn Your Hobby Into a Business." Retrieved September 01, 2016, from http://articles.bplans.com/how-to-turn-your-hobby-into-a-business/

Lorette, K. (n.d.). What Do You Need to Start a Lead Generation Company? Retrieved September 14, 2016, from http://smallbusiness.chron.com/need-start-lead-generation-company-1378.html

McClure, B. (2004). Mergers and Acquisitions: Definition | Investopedia. Retrieved September 29, 2016, from http://www.investopedia.com/university/mergers/mergers1.asp

McGoldrick, M. (n.d.). Family Systems Perspective. Retrieved September 12, 2016, from https://www.uky.edu/Classes/FAM/357/fam544/Family_Systems_Perspective.htm

Nightingale., T. (2008, June 09). "Breaking through the clutter means taking a creative chance." Retrieved September 13, 2016, from http://adage.com/article/btob/breaking-clutter-means-taking-a-creative-chance/271628/

Priesler, A. (2015). Write Your Way to a Win: Business Proposal 101. Retrieved September 26, 2016, from http://www.business.com/business-planning/write-your-way-to-a-win-business-proposal-101/

Roberts, M. J. (2004, December 1). How Venture Capitalists Evaluate Potential Venture Opportunities. *Harvard Business Publishing*.

Scalability Definition | Investopedia. (2007). Retrieved August 23, 2016, from http://www.investopedia.com/terms/s/scalability.asp#ixzz4IB27If15

"Small Business/Self-Employed Topics" (n.d.). Retrieved September 13, 2016, from https://www.irs.gov/businesses/small-businesses-self-employed/do-you-need-an-ein

"The Stages in Venture Capital Investing" - CFA Level 1 | Investopedia. (2008). Retrieved September 22, 2016, from http://www.investopedia.com/exam-guide/cfa-level-1/alternative-investments/venture-capital-investing-stages.asp

"The Top 6 Benefits Of Starting A Home-Based Business." (n.d.). Retrieved August 02, 2016, from http://www.forbes.com/sites/investopedia/2011/06/27/the-top-6-benefits-of-starting-a-home-based-business/#643774af5ed9

"Trade secret" (n.d.). Retrieved September 29, 2016, from

https://www.law.cornell.edu/wex/trade_secret

"U.S. Copyright Office Definitions" (n.d.). Retrieved September 29, 2016, from http://www.copyright.gov/help/faq/definitions.html

"What is Crowdfunding? Clear, Simple Answer Here." (2014). Retrieved September 21, 2016, from https://www.fundable.com/learn/resources/guides/crowdfunding-guide/what-is-crowdfunding